"This is another great book of expositions by Iain Duguid. In this unfolding of the armor of God, he shows us not only his well-known exegetical skills and accessible writing style but also his pastoral wisdom. This comes from both years in ministry and acquaintance with spiritual classics."

Timothy Keller, Founding Pastor, Redeemer Presbyterian Church, New York City; Chairman and Cofounder, Redeemer City to City

"Here is a rare find! This is the work of an Old Testament scholar with an easy-to-read and engaging style who believes in the ongoing activity of the evil one and writes about spiritual warfare with pastoral wisdom and biblical sanity. He knows that the battle in which we engage and the armor God supplies for us are not ideas dreamed up by the apostle Paul but were deeply embedded in the long narrative of the Old Testament. And he knows that the Lord Jesus himself faced the enemy and field-tested the armor for us. So here is a much-needed book, a battle manual for every Christian to use, and a guide for every pastor to follow."

Sinclair B. Ferguson, Chancellor's Professor of Systematic Theology, Reformed Theological Seminary; Teaching Fellow, Ligonier Ministries

"A typical nightmare for a soldier is being unarmed and undressed on the battlefield. Drawing upon decades of academic and pastoral ministry, Iain Duguid explains why Christ himself is our armor and how, paradoxically, we can only win the battle through the victory he's already achieved. Along the way, he also opens up wide vistas on how we are to live as battling victors. Highly recommended for personal, family, or group Bible study."

Michael Horton, J. Gresham Machen Professor of Systematic Theology and Apologetics, Westminster Seminary California; author, *Justification* (New Studies in Dogmatics)

"It is a joy to fervently commend this faithful and accessible treatment of Ephesians 6:10–20 by Iain Duguid. It is a powerful, gospel-saturated, Christ-exalting, and disciple-making volume that passionately calls us onward as Christian soldiers, fully dressed in the Christ-secured, Bible-defined, and Holy Spirit-delivered 'whole armor of God.'"

Harry L. Reeder III, Senior Pastor, Briarwood Presbyterian Church, Birmingham, Alabama; author, *From Embers to a Flame*; *The Leadership Dynamic*; and *3*

"I like Iain Duguid's exposition for what he avoids. He doesn't drive me to futility, nor does he allow me a cop-out. Duguid sees the gospel lurking in everything Scripture demands of us. In each of these expositions, he places us in the hands of our Redeemer. What more could one ask of an author?"

Dale Ralph Davis, Former Minister in Residence, First Presbyterian Church, Columbia, South Carolina; author, *The Word Became Fresh* and *The Message of Daniel*

THE WHOLE
ARMOR OF GOD

TRUTHFORLIFE®

THE BIBLE-TEACHING MINISTRY OF **ALISTAIR BEGG**

The mission of Truth For Life is to teach the Bible with clarity and relevance so that unbelievers will be converted, believers will be established, and local churches will be strengthened.

Daily Program

Each day, Truth For Life distributes the Bible teaching of Alistair Begg across the U.S. and in several locations outside of the U.S. through 1,800 radio outlets. To find a radio station near you, visit **truthforlife. org/stationfinder**.

Free Teaching

The daily program, and Truth For Life's entire teaching archive of over 2,000 Bible-teaching messages, can be accessed for free online and through Truth For Life's full-feature mobile app. Download the free mobile app at **truthforlife.org/app** and listen free online at **truthforlife.org**.

At-Cost Resources

Books and full-length teaching from Alistair Begg on CD, DVD, and USB are available for purchase at cost, with no markup. Visit **truthforlife.org/store**.

Where to Begin?

If you're new to Truth For Life and would like to know where to begin listening and learning, find starting point suggestions at **truthforlife. org/firststep**. For a full list of ways to connect with Truth For Life, visit **truthforlife.org/subscribe**.

Contact Truth For Life

P.O. Box 398000 Cleveland, Ohio 44139
phone 1 (888) 588-7884   **email** letters@truthforlife.org
 /truthforlife   @truthforlife   **truthforlife.org**

THE WHOLE ARMOR OF GOD

*How Christ's Victory
Strengthens Us for
Spiritual Warfare*

Iain M. Duguid

WHEATON, ILLINOIS

Trade paperback ISBN: 978-1-4335-6500-7
ePub ISBN: 978-1-4335-6503-8
PDF ISBN: 978-1-4335-6501-4
Mobipocket ISBN: 978-1-4335-6502-1

Library of Congress Cataloging-in-Publication Data

Names: Duguid, Iain M., author.
Title: The whole armor of God : how Christ's victory strengthens us for spiritual warfare / Iain M. Duguid.
Description: Wheaton : Crossway, 2019. | Includes bibliographical references and index.
Identifiers: LCCN 2019004436 (print) | LCCN 2019021799 (ebook) | ISBN 9781433565014 (pdf) | ISBN 9781433565021 (mobi) | ISBN 9781433565038 (epub) | ISBN 9781433565007 (tp)
Subjects: LCSH: Bible. Ephesians, VI, 10-13—Criticism, interpretation, etc. | Spiritual warfare—Biblical teaching.
Classification: LCC BS2695.6.S67 (ebook) | LCC BS2695.6.S67 D84 2019 (print) | DDC 227/.506—dc23
LC record available at https://lccn.loc.gov/2019004436

Crossway is a publishing ministry of Good News Publishers.

VP   29   28   27   26   25   24
15   14   13   12   11   10   9   8   7   6   5

CONTENTS

1   Dressed for Battle 9

2   The Belt of Truth 25

3   The Breastplate of Righteousness 37

4   Gospel Boots 51

5   The Shield of Faith 65

6   The Helmet of Salvation 77

7   The Sword of the Spirit 89

8   Praying Always 103

Acknowledgments 119

General Index 121

Scripture Index 125

DRESSED FOR BATTLE

Ephesians 6:10–13

Over recent years, there have been many television shows aimed at helping people get properly dressed. Sometimes the premise revolves around watching experts help people to pick the right outfit for a wedding. At other times, someone with a woefully poor fashion sense receives a total makeover with the help of fashion gurus and serious spending. As someone who is no expert in clothing trends, I find such programs fascinating. However, I would like to see follow-up programs six months later. Were the people's lives genuinely transformed by their new fashion insights, or have they reverted to their old habits, redonning saggy spandex and sandals with socks?

Christianity is a religion about helping people become properly dressed, although not in the sartorial sense. Sins against fashion ought not to be held against you in the community of believers. But Paul advises the Ephesians that there are certain things Christians must put off and others they must put on, just like in the television shows. More specifically, he tells us to put on the Christian armor so that we can be properly equipped to stand up to the assaults that will inevitably come our way in this fallen and spiritually dangerous world.

Life here on earth is hard—often very, very hard. According to the Bible, life is not a picnic but a *battle*, an armed struggle against a powerful adversary. To engage in that battle properly, we need a spiritual makeover in which our flimsy, inadequate natural attire is replaced by suitable armor and weaponry. So Paul concludes this magnificent, gospel-saturated letter, Ephesians, with a final charge to be prepared to engage with the battle of life in the right way.

In this book, we are going to unpack each of the pieces of armor he describes, but first we shall look at three perspectives that orient us to the larger fight: the scale of our need, the vastness of God's provision, and the call to stand.

THE SCALE OF OUR NEED

Paul spares no effort in describing the seriousness of our opposition. We don't wrestle with flesh and blood but against the rulers, the authorities, the cosmic powers of this present darkness (Eph. 6:12). If that sounds scary, it is because it is meant to. The devil is a very real, very powerful opponent, far too powerful for us to take on in our own strength. This is a salutary reminder to people in our Western context, who are inclined to ridicule the idea of a literal devil. Many find the idea of a cosmic being whom we can't see, feel, or touch and who promotes evil in this world unthinkable. Of course, the devil in whom they don't believe is, in their minds, often not the biblical figure but a rather ridiculous image

with hooves and horns. Who could seriously believe in that creature? It is convenient for the devil when people don't believe in
his existence. Then he can pursue his nefarious schemes unsus-
pected and undetected.

Yet who doubts the reality of evil in this universe? Almost everyone agrees that some things are not merely tragic but genuinely evil. Gassing millions of Jews in the death camps of Poland
is evil. Press-ganging young African children into an army, getting
them high on drugs, and then sending them into battle is evil. Traf-
ficking women in the sex industry is evil. Where does all this evil
in the world come from? Man's natural inhumanity to man hardly
seems a sufficient explanation for evil on this scale. Is it possible
that there is another factor, a supernatural spiritual dimension,
to all of this moral depravity? If you believe that the universe you
see around you is all there is, then you have no rational basis on
which to be shocked and outraged at evil. What we call "evil" must
then be interpreted simply as an emotional response within us to
dangerous things, triggered by evolutionary biology. But the Bible
has a richer and deeper explanation for the sad world we find ourselves in, an explanation that allows us to recognize the profound
reality of evil and the invisible spiritual forces that lie behind its
constant reappearance in different shapes and forms.

The Ephesians to whom Paul was writing were not modern
materialists. They were very well aware of the spiritual forces
around them, as people in other parts of the world continue to be.
Yet even to them, Paul makes a point of highlighting the power of
the opposition we face:

> We do not wrestle against flesh and blood, but against the rul-
> ers, against the authorities, against the cosmic powers over
> this present darkness. (Eph. 6:12)

Some of the terms that Paul uses here may have been in use in Ephesus as titles for various spiritual beings; Ephesus was a hotbed of occult interest, as Acts 19:18–19 makes clear.[1] To these people, already convinced of Satan's reality, Paul strongly underlines the power of the opposition that faced them—the same power that faces us. To use Peter's language, Satan "prowls around like a roaring lion, seeking someone to devour" (1 Pet. 5:8).

Of course, adding to the imbalance in this wrestling match is the fact that although our opponents are not flesh and blood, we are. We are not principalities and powers or cosmic rulers but ordinary flawed, fallen, flesh-and-blood mortals. You might think that we have no business engaging in this combat; in the language of Tolkien's *Lord of the Rings*, it is hobbits against orcs, an unequal contest. Yet this is exactly the battle in which we are engaged. Serving in the Lord's army is not an option reserved for those particularly devoted to God. The choice is not whether you will be a Christian soldier or a Christian civilian but whether you will be a prepared Christian soldier or an unprepared one. And an unprepared soldier of flesh and blood will not be able to stand against the scale of the spiritual forces ranged against him or her.

What is more, this conflict takes place in the midst of "this darkness." In many respects, the dark world in which we live is Satan's playground. There are tempting sights, sounds, and tastes in this world that dazzle and allure us into sin. There is much around us that seems desirable and many powerful temptations that find a ready ally in our flesh. Earthly objects are very real to us, while heavenly realities seem ethereal and intangible. Satan also has centuries of experience as a tempter, knowing exactly

---

1. See Clinton E. Arnold, *Power and Magic: The Concept of Power in Ephesians* (Grand Rapids, MI: Baker, 1992), 14.

which temptations are most likely to draw our individual human nature into sin, whether giving ourselves to a particular form of excess or to a subtle self-exalting pride that flows from a belief in our own righteousness. The powerful combination of the world, the flesh, and the devil is inevitably overwhelming, left to ourselves. This is why Paul doesn't merely say, "Bring the armor of God along with you on the off chance that you might need it." Rather, he says, "You will need it; so put it on."

As a skilled tempter, Satan also knows how to use the difficulty of the combat to his own advantage. As a child, I used to watch the science fiction program *Dr. Who*. Some of the doctor's opponents I particularly remember from those early days were the Cybermen. These terrifying bionic creatures loudly proclaimed, "Resistance is useless," sending me scurrying behind the sofa week after week. In the same way, the devil often seeks to frighten us into submission, shouting at us, "Resistance is useless!" He pretends to even greater power than he has, presenting a particular temptation to us as utterly irresistible. He says to you: "You can't help yourself. It's the way you were made. You need this sin to be happy. What is the point of resisting? You know you are going to lose in the end, so you might as well just give in now."

THE SCALE OF GOD'S PROVISION

To combat this strategy, we need to understand the scale of the provision God has given us. Paul's desire is that we should be able to stand against the schemes of the devil, and to that end he begins by outlining God's far greater power. Even before he introduces the opposition forces, Paul tells us that we are to be strong in God's awesome, magnificent power, a power that is beyond compare. The words Paul uses here in Ephesians 6:10 are an echo of the same Greek words that he used in 1:19 to describe the power of God that raised up Christ.[2] In other words, the power with which we have been equipped for our struggle against sin and Satan is the very same power that brought Christ back from the dead.

This is not just the power that would be required to raise someone like Lazarus from the dead (see John 11:1–44). Raising the physically dead is no big deal, comparatively speaking. Yet the power of God is great enough to raise *Christ* from the dead, Jesus Christ who was buried in death under the full weight of God's wrath against sin—the sin of every one of his people throughout all ages, including you and me. This power of God not only raised Jesus Christ back to life but lifted him to the heavenly realms, so that he is now seated at the right hand of the Father in glory. There is real power, far greater even than the terrifying power ranged against us! The one who is in us is greater than the one who is in the world (1 John 4:4).

SELF-DIRECTED SANCTIFICATION?

That brings us to the call to stand. Paul says, "Be strong in the Lord. . . . Put on the whole armor of God, that you may be able to stand against the schemes of the devil" (Eph. 6:10–11). What many of us hear in these words is a call to triumphant action, as if it is completely up to us to take on the devil and withstand his schemes. If we would just put on the whole armor of God, we should therefore constantly be able to stand firm against all of Satan's schemes. God has done his part perfectly in making the armor available; now it is up to us to choose whether to use it. Meanwhile, God appears helpless in heaven, waiting to see

---

2. The ESV's "Be strong" and "the strength of his might" represent three Greek words: *endunamoo, kratos,* and *ischus.*

how it all turns out. When this wrong understanding holds sway, Christians get sorted into one of two camps. Some choose to be radical disciples of Jesus and live an epic life by putting on that armor. Others, by their neglect, become those "loser" Christians who are regularly tripped up by the devil's schemes, falling into sin daily, leaving God perpetually disappointed. In reality, many of us find ourselves daily in the second category: we are often unwilling and unable even to think clearly about the armor, let alone put it on. If sanctification were as simple as some suggest ("Just try harder to put on the armor!"), we would not fail and fall in the Christian life nearly as much as we do. Not for nothing does the Heidelberg Catechism remind us that even the holiest men (and women) make only "small beginnings" on the road to obedience in this life.[3]

An inevitable result of this self-focused perspective on our spiritual growth is that we become proud of ourselves and judgmental of others if we think that we are doing well in our struggle against sin and Satan. After all, *we* chose to put on God's armor while they made poor choices. Alternatively, we feel utterly crushed if we are all too aware of our frequent failures and compromises with the world, the flesh, and the devil. Perhaps we find ourselves riding an emotional roller coaster between those two extremes: ecstatic and happy when we succeed in our battles against sin but depressed and anxious when we all too often fail.

In reality, God's awesome power is not something we can choose to tap into, as if we were in charge of the process; rather, it is something inevitably at work within all those whom God has chosen and called according to his purpose. At the beginning of his letter to the Ephesians, Paul reminds us that God predestined

---

3. Heidelberg Catechism, answer 114.

us before the foundation of the world to be holy and blameless in his sight, according to the good pleasure of his will, so that we should be for the praise of his glorious grace (Eph. 1:4–6). God hasn't left it up to us to decide whether that purpose will succeed! No, his mighty power is at work for every believer in Christ to accomplish his ultimate purpose of presenting us to himself holy and blameless, to the praise of his glory. As Paul said in Philippians 2:13, it is *God* who is at work in us, both to will and to work for his good purpose.

That mighty power of God is at work for our spiritual growth in two distinct ways. First, it was demonstrated outside us in the once-for-all work of Christ in resisting sin and Satan in our place; and, second, it is demonstrated inside us through the ongoing, progressive work of the Spirit, renewing our hearts and minds. In both these ways, God is sovereign over the whole process of sanctifying his church from start to finish. There will be nothing in which any of us can boast on that last day.

THE ARMOR OF GOD IS GOD'S ARMOR

Let's unpack that idea in connection with God's armor. Our sanctification rests first and foremost on the finished work of Christ in our place. As we shall see, the armor of God is quite literally God's armor—armor designed for and worn by God first and foremost. The armor God gives us to defend and protect us against Satan's onslaught is the armor that he has already worn in the decisive battle on our behalf. We fight and stand firm against Satan only in the strength that comes from the victory that Christ has already won for us.

That is why each of the various pieces of armor points us to Christ. The belt of truth is the belt that girds the messianic king in Isaiah 11:5. The breastplate of righteousness and the helmet of salvation come from the divine warrior's arsenal in Isaiah 59:17. The feet shod with gospel readiness are the feet of those who proclaim the arrival of Messiah's kingdom in Isaiah 52:7. God himself is the shield of faith, as he describes himself in Genesis 15. The sword of the Spirit, the Word of God, is the weapon wielded by the promised servant of the Lord in Isaiah 49:2.

What God clothes us with is nothing less than his own armor, the same armor that Christ has already worn on our behalf in his lifelong struggle with the mortal enemy of our souls, Satan himself. Unlike armchair generals who watch the fighting from a safe distance, Jesus has himself worn the armor and won the victory. You are called to wear the armor of God not because that's what Jesus would do if he found himself in a similar situation; you are called to wear God's armor because that is what Jesus has already done, wearing God's armor all the way to the cross. He stood firm against Satan's schemes throughout his earthly life and ministry. Each of those specific temptations to which we have given in this week—lust, gossip, anger, pride, self-exaltation, lying, coveting—are temptations he faced and stared down in your place. What is more, Jesus laid his life down for you in winning the victory that lets loose God's sanctifying Spirit in your life. Because of his victorious life, death, and resurrection, the same power that raised Christ up from the dead is now at work inside you and me through the ongoing work of the Spirit, raising us from spiritual death to new life. However, that ongoing work of the Spirit in your life is ultimately no more under our control than God's first work of regenerating us.[4] In

---

4. See Westminster Confession of Faith 16.3: "[Christians'] ability to do good works is not at all of themselves, but wholly from the Spirit of Christ. And that they must be enabled thereunto, beside the graces they have already received, there is required an actual

John 3, Jesus compares the process of becoming a Christian to birth. Just as a baby doesn't have control over the time and circumstances of her birth, so God chose when to regenerate you and bring you to faith in Christ. Even after a child is born, she cannot choose to grow or not to grow. She may wish to be taller or shorter, but wishing won't make it so. In the same way, we are not in control of the process of our spiritual growth. The God who has started a good work in us *will* bring it to completion on the day of Christ Jesus (Phil. 1:6). Even though we are not passive but are to fight with all our might, our sanctification is ultimately God's work from beginning to end.

That perspective is enormously encouraging in our daily struggle with sin and Satan. We often imagine we are fighting alone in our struggles against sin. Not at all. Your victory over sin belongs to Jesus, not you. Jesus's struggle was the decisive one, not yours. His victory on the cross purchased your complete sanctification, your ultimate holiness before God. His Spirit is at work within you growing you at the rate that he intends toward his goal of your complete purity. Your sanctification is where he plans for it to be.

That doesn't mean that we'll never have to struggle with sin, of course. Quite the reverse: Paul clearly expects us to be engaged in a daily life-and-death struggle with Satan in all of his awesome power. The imagery of armor and battle shows us that the fight against sin must involve blood, sweat, and tears. Philippians 2:12–13 tells us to work out our own salvation *because* God is at work in us. But Christ's victory over sin at the cross means that your struggle against sin is never hopeless. God will ultimately sanctify you—he has promised to do so. On that last day, you

influence of the same Holy Spirit, to work in them to will and to do, of his good pleasure."
Compare the similar emphasis in the Canons of the Synod of Dordt 5.4.

will rise to new life in Christ and stand in God's presence, made perfect forever. Sin and Satan shall not have ultimate dominion over you.

This means that in the midst of the pain of the frustrating daily struggle against sin and Satan, you can plead with God to continue to advance that process here and now. It gives you hope to keep on trying, even in areas of your life where sin continually seems to have the upper hand. It means that when you are seeing real advance in your life, you will know that it is nothing you have accomplished. God's Holy Spirit deserves the glory, not you.

THE GLORY OF OUR WEAKNESS

Indeed, in pursuit of glory, the Spirit often turns us over to ourselves to show us just how weak we really are. You can see this in the life of King Hezekiah. He had walked with God for many years and seen much of God's goodness to him. But in 2 Chronicles 32:21, we are told that God left Hezekiah to himself, to uncover what was in his heart. The result was his greatest sin, proudly showing the Babylonians around his treasuries in an effort to persuade them that he could be a good ally against the Assyrians. This explains the puzzling nature of our struggle. We often assume that since God is holy and hates sin, his primary goal is that we should always stand strong in our battle against sin. However, the Spirit has no interest in turning us into independent creatures who can stand in our own strength.[5] Rather, he wants us to see clearly the reality that we have no power within ourselves to take up God's armor and stand, unless God himself empowers us to do that. We are called to "be strong in the Lord" (Eph. 6:10), not to be strong in ourselves. Left to ourselves, we will certainly

---

5. On this, see John Newton, "The Advantages of Remaining Sin," in *Select Letters of John Newton* (Edinburgh: Banner of Truth, 2011), 150–55.

fall to the schemes of the devil. As the Westminster Confession of Faith puts it:

> The most wise, righteous, and gracious God doth oftentimes leave, for a season, his own children to manifold temptations, and the corruption of their own hearts, to chastise them for their former sins, or to discover unto them the hidden strength of corruption and deceitfulness of their hearts, that they may be humbled; and, to raise them to a more close and constant dependence for their support upon himself, and to make them more watchful against all future occasions of sin, and for sundry other just and holy ends.[6]

Did you catch what the confession is saying? The confession says that the righteous and holy God *often* leaves his own children in the grip of manifold temptations, experiencing the corruption of their own hearts, for his own holy purposes. He desires above all that we would grow in humility and dependence upon his grace. The confession accurately describes our experience. We learn the depravity of our own sinful nature, the vast superiority of Satan's skill, our constant need of Christ's perfect sacrifice, and the ongoing power of the Holy Spirit within us most often through our experience of our own sin and failure rather than during our few moments of spiritual triumph. As John Newton would say, we don't learn of the depth of the corruption of our nature simply by being told it; we learn it through bitter experience as we struggle with sins that seem as natural as breathing—and as hard to give up.[7]

Nothing teaches us the power of Satan or our utter dependence upon God more than our constant spiritual failures. If I

---

6. Westminster Confession of Faith 5.5.
7. See John Newton, "The Advantages of Remaining Sin," 153.

make repeated resolutions to give up a certain sin, and I fast and pray and still find myself giving in to it, what else can I conclude but that I am indeed the weakest of Christians? When I resolve over and over not to say the unkind and prideful words that repeatedly spring into my mind, but still find myself hurting people and exalting myself regularly, what shall I say except, "Wretched man that I am! Who will deliver me from this body of death?" (Rom. 7:24).

Nothing gives us more passion for the righteousness of Christ than a specific and growing awareness of our own brokenness. When I am strong and living the Christian life well, I may be fond of the gospel as a concept, but when I see more clearly the ongoing depth of my sinfulness, then I cling to the gospel like a drowning man to a life belt. Nothing gives us a greater desire for the completion of the Spirit's work on the last day, and our full deliverance from the battle against this body of death, than those times when the conflict with remaining sin in our lives is at its fiercest.

Those who are not yet believers in Christ are often comfortable with their sin; for them, there really is no struggle. But when God begins to work, people start to see the ugliness of their own heart, and they begin to sense their need of a redeemer—someone to rescue them from themselves. Jesus is precisely that Redeemer, who both fights the battle in their place and then engages the battle inside and alongside them through the powerful work of his Holy Spirit.

Life is a battle for Christians; Jesus told his disciples to take up their cross (Matt. 16:24), not to take up their armchair. We are engaged in conflict against an enemy whose strength and skill far outmatch our own. But it is a battle that we have been equipped to fight in the sure knowledge that we've been enlisted on the winning side. We take up our cross because our Savior first took up his. We wear God's armor because Jesus wore it first. In the final analysis, standing our ground simply means clinging desperately to Jesus Christ as our only hope of salvation. In that attitude of dependent trust is true victory. For all of his power and wiles, Satan has no ability to snatch away those who are trusting in Christ, for they are the children of God, and their Father will not let them go. They have been entrusted by the Father into the safe keeping of the Son and are indwelt by the Spirit himself.

Everything you need for your salvation has been accomplished for you by Jesus Christ, and he himself is now working in you by his Spirit to work out that salvation. Sometimes God will demonstrate his power in you by enabling you to stand strong against Satan's devices; at other times, his purpose is graciously to allow you to fall to teach you equally important lessons about your own weakness and the glorious sufficiency of his grace to save and sustain the weakest of the weak. Either way, the glory will all be his on the last day.

So "be strong in the Lord and in the strength of his might"; take your stand against the devil, protected by the armor that God has provided. Fight the good fight with all your might. Wrestle with all the energy that the Spirit gives you. But in the midst of that standing, fighting, and wrestling, don't forget to rest in the finished victory of Christ and the assurance that the Spirit's perfect sanctifying work in your life is what counts.

FOR FURTHER REFLECTION

1. Do you believe that life is a battle? How have you experienced that reality recently?

2. Do you take seriously the reality of Satan's role in the conflict? How does that impact the way you approach difficult situations?

3. Does Satan more effectively tempt you by showing you the seductive attractiveness of sin or by threatening to overpower you? How have you experienced these different modes of temptation?

4. Why does it matter that the power God has equipped us with is the same power that raised Christ from the dead?

5. What difference does it make to the sanctification process if we really believe that it is God's work from beginning to end? Why is it important that Jesus wore spiritual armor first?

2

THE BELT OF TRUTH

Ephesians 6:14

The British have a passion for talking about the weather. One reason for the habit could be that the weather in Britain is often changeable. If you don't like the climate, wait a while, and it will show you something different. Sometimes you might be able to experience all four seasons in the course of a single day. When I lived in Edinburgh, the locals had a saying that summed up the climate. If when you stood on the ramparts of Edinburgh Castle and looked north, you could see all the way across the Firth of Forth, then it was going to rain. If you couldn't, the chances were it was already raining. Sooner or later—and probably sooner rather than later—you could count on it raining in Edinburgh, so you had better keep an umbrella handy.

According to Paul, one of the other certainties in life is that sooner or later—and probably sooner rather than later—you are going to experience the attacks of the devil. Life as a Christian is not a picnic. It is an armed struggle against a powerful opponent, so you need to be properly dressed in the armor that God has provided.

BEGINNING WITH THE BELT OF TRUTH

Paul itemizes the armor piece by piece. The first component he mentions is the belt of truth. The belt was the logical place to start because it was the first piece of the soldier's equipment to be strapped on. It went underneath the armor to hold all the other clothing out of the way. In those days, when people wore long, flowing robes, the belt enabled a person to run and fight without being encumbered. To update the image, it is challenging to fight if your pants keep falling down. The belt is foundational to any soldier's effectiveness, and, according to Paul, the equivalent of the belt in God's armor is truth. Truth is essential to the Christian life; it is foundational to taking a stand against the devil.

The Christian message unambiguously claims to be *the* truth, not just *a* truth. In the contemporary world, there are some who say, "It doesn't matter what you believe, as long as you're sincere. You believe one thing about God, I believe another, but we're all essentially approaching the same God from different sides." In reality, people who say, "It doesn't matter what you believe about God as long as you are sincere," are those to whom it doesn't matter what you believe about God. But if there is a God who designed the whole cosmic and human story with a purpose, so that the chief end of man is to glorify this God and enjoy him forever, then what you believe about God becomes a matter of supreme and decisive importance.

The Bible unambiguously declares that it matters what you believe. Christianity, according to the Bible, is not simply one way among many of getting to God; it is the truth. Jesus Christ is the only pathway through whom we may approach the Father. The apostle Peter declared, "There is salvation in no one else, for there is no other name under heaven given among men by which we must be saved" (Acts 4:12). Paul said something similar in Ephesians 1:13, where he declares that the gospel of salvation is "the word of truth." In Ephesians 4:21, Paul contrasts Christianity to the pagan approach to life that the Ephesians had previously followed, saying, "You were taught in him [that is, in Jesus] as the truth is in Jesus." Here Paul is not contrasting the truth that is in Jesus with the truth that is in Confucius or the truth that is in Islam. No, Paul is contrasting the truth that is in Jesus as opposed to the darkened understanding that is the universal trademark of the non-Christian way of life.

In this, of course, Paul was simply following Jesus's own words, when he said, "I am the way, and the truth, and the life. No one comes to the Father except through me" (John 14:6). Christianity claims loudly to be the truth. And the truth with which we are to be belted in order to face up to the devil is, first and foremost, the truth of what we believe: the gospel message of who God is, who we are, and what he requires of us as created human beings. This truth is revealed to us in the Word of God, the Scriptures.

WEARING THE BELT OF TRUTH

A belt is no help to you hanging in your closet; you have to put it on. Similarly, truth is of no value to you hanging unused in God's Word. You need to put it on. You need to become adept at connecting the Bible to your life. Listen to what James says in his letter:

> But be doers of the word and not hearers only, deceiving yourselves. For if anyone is a hearer of the word and not a doer, he is like a man who looks intently at his natural face in a mirror.

For he looks at himself and goes away and at once forgets what he was like. But the one who looks into the perfect law, the law of liberty, and perseveres, being no hearer who forgets but a doer who acts, he will be blessed in his doing. (James 1:22–25)

That's the reason many Christians set aside a particular time during the day to read the Bible and pray. We don't do it to prove our spirituality to God. We do it because it is a good way to grab hold of truth, as we read the Bible, and then in prayer to wrestle with how to apply that truth to our lives. The measure of that time of study and prayer is not, "Did it leave me with a warm glow all over?" Rather, it is, "Did it equip me with truth? Is there some aspect of God's Word that I now understand better, which I can now use more effectively in my life?"

That's one reason why, when you try to set aside a few minutes to read the Bible, you will find that that time will be the special object of the devil's attention. He will bring to mind all the distractions he can. You will suddenly think of all the things you need to do—all those things that at other times slip by unremembered. All your appointments for the day and the items on your to-do list are immediately presented for your attention. The Internet suddenly seems overwhelmingly attractive. You feel an urgent need to check your email or even to go to the gym! Does that problem sound familiar? The devil hates truth and will do anything he can to distract you from it. Indeed, the Bible says that Satan has been a liar from the beginning (John 8:44). That is how he persuaded Adam and Eve to sin in the first place, with a lie: "Did God actually say, 'You shall not eat from any tree in the garden'?" (Gen. 3:1). What God actually said was, "You may surely eat of every tree of the garden, but of the tree of the knowledge of good and evil you shall not eat" (2:16–17). Satan lied, and Adam and Eve listened to his lie—like the rest of us so often do—with all of the tragic consequences that followed.

ANSWERING SATAN WITH THE TRUTH

The devil wants to persuade you to believe a lie. As a result, he will go to extraordinary lengths to limit your contact with God's Word, which is the truth. Once he's separated you from truth, he starts with his perverse words: "God doesn't have your best interests at heart. He is out to spoil your fun. If you are a Christian, your life will be miserable because God's laws restrict your freedom. Sin is the way to true happiness and fulfillment." Those are lies of the devil. And the truth with which to answer them effectively is found in the Bible.

Is obedience to God's law a misery? On the contrary, the psalmist tells us:

> The law of the LORD is perfect,
>   reviving the soul;
> the testimony of the LORD is sure,
>   making wise the simple;
> the precepts of the LORD are right,
>   rejoicing the heart;
> the commandment of the LORD is pure,
>   enlightening the eyes;
> the fear of the LORD is clean,
>   enduring forever;
> the rules of the LORD are true,
>   and righteous altogether.
> More to be desired are they than gold,
>   even much fine gold;
> sweeter also than honey
>   and drippings of the honeycomb.

Moreover, by them is your servant warned;
in keeping them there is great reward. (Ps. 19:7–11)

Does God not have our best interests at heart? Romans 8:28–31 gives the answer to that:

> We know that for those who love God all things work together for good, for those who are called according to his purpose. For those whom he foreknew he also predestined to be conformed to the image of his Son, in order that he might be the firstborn among many brothers. And those whom he predestined he also called, and those whom he called he also justified, and those whom he justified he also glorified. What then shall we say to these things? If God is for us, who can be against us?

The Bible gives us truth with which we can answer the devil and thus stand firm against his schemes. But like a belt, in order for that truth to do us any good, we have to bind it around us afresh every day. Our hearts are leaky containers, constantly losing our hold on the truth. Day by day, we need to refill our mind with a fresh measure of God's truth, revealed in the Scriptures, so that we will be equipped to stand against Satan's lies.

A SYSTEM OF TRUTH

What the Bible gives to us, however, is not simply little nuggets of truth—one truth over here, another truth over there—but rather a whole system of teaching, of doctrine. All the different parts of the Bible are related and interrelated, and when you put them together as a whole, they teach us what we must believe about God and what God requires of us.

The idea of doctrine is not very popular in our day and age. People don't want someone telling them what they should believe or what they should do. Even Christians can fall into that way of thinking. "Let's not talk about doctrine," they say. "Doctrine divides us. Let's talk about our experiences instead. Experiences unite us." Unfortunately, what these people fail to realize is that they too are pushing a doctrine: the doctrine that doctrine doesn't matter. Their doctrine is that experience is what counts! In reality, you can't get away from having doctrine. Everybody—even atheists—have a system of beliefs about who God is and what he requires of man. Your belief may be that God is irrelevant and that he demands nothing of man. Or you may think of God as a stern judge who will zap anyone who fails to give absolute and immediate obedience. But whatever you believe, you inevitably have a system of doctrine that explains what you believe about God and what he requires of man. G. K. Chesterton put it like this:

> Men have always one of two things: either a complete and conscious philosophy or the unconscious acceptance of the broken bits of some incomplete and often discredited philosophy. . . . Philosophy is merely thought that has been thought out. It is often a great bore. But man has no alternative, except between being influenced by thought that has been thought out and being influenced by thought that has not been thought out.[1]

If everybody has their own system of doctrine, the key question becomes: Is your system of doctrine the truth? There are right answers and wrong answers to the questions, "Who is God?" and "What does he want from me?" In my capacity as a seminary professor, I set many exams. Sadly, not all the students do equally well. Generally the problem is not that the students are insincere about their answers. Rather, it is that they sincerely

---

1. G. K. Chesterton, *The Common Man* (New York: Sheed & Ward, 1950), 173.

believed something totally wrong! It's the same way with life. Many people are going through life sincerely believing all the wrong answers about who God is and what he wants from humanity. But it doesn't have to be that way. God has given us the answers to those questions in the Bible. Suppose that in one of my exams, I handed out a book containing all the answers along with the test. How many of my students would say, "I don't believe in being indoctrinated with *your* answers. I think I'll make up my own answers"? How foolish that would be! Yet how many people go through life similarly ignoring God's answer book, the Bible?

Where did you get your ideas about who God is and what he wants from you? Perhaps you formulated them for yourself. Or perhaps you are relying on what your parents told you or some other person in authority. From wherever you got your ideas, you have the ability to check out whether they are right or wrong because in the Bible you have access to the truth! You can find out for yourself the message about the all-powerful, sovereign God who created this world out of nothing. You may learn the truth about Jesus, the infinite God-man—the One who was God from all eternity and who took on humanity for us. You can discover the reason that Jesus became man, so that he could live the perfect life in our place and die in our place on the cross so that we might receive his perfect goodness, while all our awful failures and brokenness could be laid upon him. The Scriptures also tell us about heaven, which God has prepared for us as a completely free gift—not something that we could earn by our efforts but something purchased for us by another. You can learn about faith, which enables us to receive that free gift and live a new life on the basis of it. Without this belt of truth, you'll be unprepared to face Satan's schemes. You will be deceived by his canny lies, held captive by his subtlety and trickery.

JESUS WORE THE BELT OF TRUTH FIRST

Wearing the armor of God is not simply a matter of doing all the right things so that we can stand firm against Satan. God is the one who strengthens us to stand, and the armor we need is fundamentally God's armor, which Jesus Christ has already worn in our place. That is great news because the reality is that we aren't very good at wearing the belt of truth as our foundation garment. We may know all kinds of things about the Bible, or about the gospel, but we still find it remarkably easy to lose our grip on the reality it reveals. We sometimes turn our study of the Bible into an academic exercise, as if we were reading to get an A on a test rather than to equip our souls for mortal combat. At other times, we may recognize clearly how a Bible passage applies to other people, while completely missing what it has to say to confront and correct us. Our weak grasp on the truth will never be enough to save us.

But God himself has entered the fray on our behalf. In Isaiah 11, God's people, Israel, had turned their back on the light and chosen to live in darkness, spurning the Lord's revelation. Yet the Lord promised that he would send a messianic figure from the line of David to deliver them. A king would come to rescue them, wearing righteousness as a belt around his waist and faithfulness as a belt around his loins (Isa. 11:5). Significantly, the Greek translation of the Old Testament renders "faithfulness" here as *aletheia*, the same Greek word that Paul uses in Ephesians 6, and which our English versions translate as "truth." Through his foundational righteousness and faithfulness to God's Word, this messianic king will save his people and bring in the final blessing of peace—a peace that extends throughout creation. The toxic effects of the fall, brought about by the first Adam listening to Satan's lies, would be reversed by this second Adam and heir of the line of David whose foundational qualities are truth and faithfulness.

Jesus demonstrated that righteousness and faithfulness to the truth in his encounters with Satan in the wilderness. Satan sought to persuade Jesus that God wouldn't provide for his needs, so Jesus should make stones into bread. Jesus replied with God's truth: "Man shall not live by bread alone, but by every word that comes from the mouth of God" (Matt. 4:4). Satan tried to get Jesus to perform a miraculous sign by throwing himself off the pinnacle of the temple. Jesus responded once again with the word of truth: "It is written, 'You shall not put the Lord your God to the test'" (Matt. 4:7). Then Satan floated the most outrageous lie of all. He showed Jesus all the kingdoms of the world and promised, "All these I will give you, if you will fall down and worship me" (Matt. 4:9). For a third time Jesus saw through the lie and responded with the truth of God's Word: "You shall worship the Lord your God and him only you shall serve" (Matt. 4:10). Jesus had belted on the Word of truth ahead of time, so when Satan assaulted him with his lies, he found Jesus thoroughly equipped to repel his assaults.

That is so different from our daily experience. Satan simply has to show us something attractive, and we go after it, even when we know it to be contrary to God's Word. The lusts of the eyes, the lusts of the flesh, the pride of life—all the things that feed our appetites, our desires, and our sense of self-importance—seduce us easily away from the truth and into sin (see 1 John 2:16). We are not equipped with a solid belt of faithfully appropriating the truth, but Jesus was, in our place. His faithful girding of himself with the truth stands for us, so that on the last day, when the Father summons us into his presence, he will not condemn us for our faithlessness but will delight to clothe us in Christ's perfect faithfulness. Even now Christ clothes us with his perfect love of the truth, as if it were our very own. What a wonderful truth that is!

The more we grasp the truth of Christ's righteousness in our place, the more this truth will strengthen us in turn against Satan's lies. If the God of the universe has chosen and called us in Christ and given us a glorious inheritance in him, that is surely better than whatever tawdry bauble Satan places under our nose. If this God is my loving Father, who works all things for my good according to his perfect plan, then I have an answer to Satan's lies about God not caring about me. If the good work God has begun in me will be brought to completion on the day of Christ Jesus, then it is worth striving with every sinew and nerve of my soul to work out that salvation now in a life of growing obedience. If my failures are meant to drive me to the cross in repentant humility, and the Father's arms are always open to welcome the returning prodigal, then Satan's claim that God will surely spurn me because of my fresh sin loses its sting. Foundational truth, belted around our waists, enables us to stand against Satan, even as it points us away from ourselves to Jesus Christ as the only one who can make us stand.

The armor of God, Christ's armor, is not a pristine, clean outfit: it is already bloodied from his fight. Christ's faithfulness took him all the way to the cross, where he won his final victory, no longer clothed in his armor but left naked and defenseless against his enemies. Even at the cross, Satan continued to throw his lies at Jesus: "This man said he was the king of the Jews" (see John 19:21–22); and, "If you are the Son of God, come down from the cross" (see Matt. 27:39–43). Yet Jesus persisted in clinging to the precious truth of his Father's continued care and love for him, even when the blackness of the sky above him seemed to tell a different story. His final words of truth on earth were, "It is finished! Father, into your hands I commit my Spirit" (see John 19:30 and Luke 23:46).

So truth won its final victory over Satan's lies. Men and women were purchased for God, even at the cost of the life of his own dear Son. Your justification, your sanctification, even your final glorification were truly accomplished in that act. In his obedient life and faithful death, your final destiny was secured, once and for all. With that truth, you have an unanswerable response to all of Satan's untruths. The belt of truth is your foundation garment. Put it on; wear it; be found in it day and night—for in Christ that truth will set you free from the grip of Satan's powerful lies.

FOR FURTHER REFLECTION

1. Why is truth so important in the Christian life?

2   What gets in the way of your accessing and believing the truth?

3. Why is it important that Jesus loved and believed the truth during his earthly life?

4. What specific truths about God, about yourself, or about the gospel do you need to grasp and remember right now?

THE BREASTPLATE OF RIGHTEOUSNESS

Isaiah 59:12–21; Ephesians 6:14

One of my favorite occupations at an international airport is to watch new arrivals and try to guess where they are from. If they are talking, I can sometimes tell from their language or accent, but I try to guess simply by what they are wearing. It is not as easy as you might think, because people don't dress according to national stereotypes. Scots don't always wear kilts. People from Germany aren't necessarily wearing lederhosen. And tourists from America don't routinely wear Hawaiian shirts and baseball caps. Actually, you rarely see anyone who matches the national stereotype, especially at an airport, where almost everyone is in either jeans or a suit, yet we still maintain a mental image of what people of a certain nationality *ought* to look like.

But what does the typical Christian look like? What part of the Christian's armor does the average person think of when she thinks about what makes someone a Christian? I don't think that it is the belt of truth, or the shoes of the gospel, or the shield of faith, or the helmet of salvation, or the sword of the Spirit, which is the Word of God, even though these things are essential to living as a properly dressed Christian. Instead, most people think of righteousness as the essential ingredient of being a Christian. That is, most non-Christians think that Christians are people who have got their life sorted out and are therefore acceptable to God—or at least that Christians *think* they have their lives sorted out. To put it another way, for many people, a Christian is someone who is (or thinks she is) a decent, moral person who lives her life in the right way.

WHAT IS THE BREASTPLATE OF RIGHTEOUSNESS?

What Paul means by the "breastplate of righteousness," however, is not a set of accomplishments that we create for ourselves; rather, it is something given to us to put on. This breastplate is not our workmanship; it is part of the armor that God provides for us, a righteousness that is not our own. Paul didn't invent the different pieces of the armor of God; they come from various passages in the Old Testament, especially the book of Isaiah. Nowhere is Paul's dependence on the Old Testament clearer than with the breastplate of righteousness and the helmet of salvation, which are both drawn directly from Isaiah 59:17.

The trouble with the popular view of what makes someone a Christian, that what gets us into God's good books are our own efforts to obey God, is that our righteousness can never be good enough. Even when I am trying to obey God, I regularly do, say, and think things that are either against what God tells me to do or not in line with what God tells me I ought to do, which is sin. What is more, the Bible says that the wages of sin is death (Rom. 6:23). That is, the reward that we deserve each and every time that we fail to obey God fully from our hearts is death, eternal separation from God. Yet we all sin many times each day.

If you fail to live up to God's perfect standard only once a day, it would come to 365 sins per year (plus one in a leap year), or almost twenty-six thousand sins in the average lifetime. And one sin a day would be a remarkable accomplishment for any of us! What positive good can we set against that? Perhaps we may have done a few good deeds here and there, but these were only the things that we should have done anyway, and often not even that much. We all have sins of omission as well as sins of commission. Indeed, even when we do the right thing, our motives for our actions are often horribly mixed, or entirely selfish.

So, then, I will earn the death penalty more than twenty-six thousand times in my lifetime, and my only defense is that some of the rest of the time, I was doing what I should have been doing. That's not much of a defense, is it? It's like someone who is caught stealing millions of dollars from his employer and excuses his behavior by saying, "Well, whenever I wasn't stealing from you, I was doing my job!" Such a person deserves punishment. So, too, we must acknowledge what each of us deserves at the hands of a perfectly holy God. We deserve to be tossed into the fire without so much as a second thought. Our own righteousness won't protect us against God, let alone against the devil.

THE DIVINE WARRIOR

Not coincidentally, that problematic situation is exactly what the prophet was addressing in Isaiah 59. In the preceding chapters,

Isaiah described God's promise to deal with the physical enemies of his people, especially Babylon. But now the prophet describes the divine warrior coming to deal with the far greater and more dangerous enemy of their souls, sin. To take on this enemy and bring about the final deliverance of his people, God put on his own armor—*his* breastplate of righteousness and *his* helmet of salvation—and he intervened to rescue them. No one else could have delivered Israel from such a powerful foe, but the Lord's mighty arm would defeat his adversaries and bring redemption to his chosen ones. His people have no righteousness of their own to bring him; indeed, the prophet declares to Israel that even their best righteousness is nothing more than filthy garments (Isa. 64:6). The people know that their iniquities have separated them from God (59:2). If the Lord were to deal with his people according to their deeds, there would be nothing to anticipate but the fearful prospect of judgment.

But the divine warrior would not come to his own people as a fearsome judge; he would come as their promised Redeemer. He would come to Zion to rescue Israel not merely from external trials and difficulties but from their sin, which separated them from him. The Lord's dramatic intervention would transform the fortunes of the nations as well as Israel's fortunes. As a result, there would be a new fear of the Lord's name in the west and of his glory in the east (Isa. 59:19). The ends of the earth would see the salvation of our God (Isa. 52:10).

Yet this promised intervention by God would be intensely costly. He could not simply redeem his people from a safe distance. In Isaiah 59:16, when the Lord observes that there is no one to intercede for his people, the Hebrew word used for "intercede" (*pana'*) is the same word that ends Isaiah 53 (v. 12).

There, the Lord spoke of the suffering servant who would win the victory and intercede for transgressors by bearing their sins himself; the Lord's decisive triumph over transgression would be won through the servant's agonizing submission to pain and disfigurement as an atoning substitute for his people.

So when Paul talks about putting on the breastplate of righteousness, he is describing the righteousness that God gives us in the gospel, about which he wrote: "For our sake he made him to be sin who knew no sin, so that in him we might become the righteousness of God" (2 Cor. 5:21). God has intervened decisively in this world to make sinners the righteousness of God. God brought about this dramatic transformation, changing us from filthy to clean, from guilty to innocent, by making him who had no sin to be sin for us. Here, Paul is simply unpacking the promise that God gave through Isaiah, that the Divine Warrior would win the victory over our sin by becoming the suffering servant who bears our transgressions in our place.

A DOUBLE TRANSFORMATION

At the heart of the Christian message are two equal and opposite transformations. Each is dramatic; each would be unbelievable if we didn't have God's own Word on it. They are these: God took Jesus, the only perfect person who ever lived, the only one who could ever stand before God on the basis of his own goodness—God's own beloved Son—and stripped off from Jesus these clean clothes of faithful obedience. The Father tore off Jesus's righteous standing before him and treated him as if he were the guilty one. He made Jesus to be blackened with our sin, our iniquity, our transgression—all the filthy thoughts, abusive words, and vile actions that you and I have committed in the past or will commit in the future.

On the cross, Jesus suffered the penalty for all those sins against God's holiness. Jesus's suffering was not just the physical agony of the nails that were pounded through living flesh and the sharp thorns that were pressed into his forehead until blood ran down his cheeks. That was just the beginning of the servant's suffering. The worst part was the spiritual pain of his separation from God. The one who had walked with God in righteousness and goodness from the beginning of time cried out in agony, "My God, my God why have you forsaken me?" (Matt. 27:46). God had forsaken him because God was treating him as guilty of sin—my sin and your sin and the sin of all his people. As Isaiah put it, he was pierced because of our rebellion; he was crushed for our iniquities. He bore the sin of many (Isa. 53:5, 12).

And then, equally remarkably, having treated the innocent one as guilty, God treats the guilty ones as innocent. Paul puts it like this: "In Christ God was reconciling the world to himself, not counting their trespasses against them" (2 Cor. 5:19). Instead of counting our sins against us, God chooses to count for us Christ's righteousness. As Isaiah had said, "Upon him was the chastisement that brought us peace, and with his wounds we are healed" (Isa. 53:5). It is not just that God doesn't count against us all the times that we have fallen short of his perfect standard; he also counts *for* us all the times Jesus faced a similar temptation and stood firm. His perfect righteousness and holy obedience are credited to our account. The robe of perfect obedience that God stripped off the back of his own Son, he now gives to clothe us (see Zechariah 3). In Christ, we have received a breastplate of righteousness that defends us forever against the wrath of God.

RIGHTEOUS IN CHRIST

This great exchange applies only to those who are united to Christ, that is, to those who are Christians. As Paul says in Romans 8, "There is therefore now no condemnation for those who are *in Christ Jesus*" (v. 1). In 2 Corinthians 5:17 he says, "If anyone is *in Christ*, he is a new creation. The old has passed away; behold, the new has come." From your perspective, you come to Jesus and bow your heart before him, saying: "I want all of the wrong things I have ever done or will do to be laid to your account, and I want your perfect righteousness to be credited to my account. Please make me part of your new creation. Reconcile me to God; make me acceptable to the Father through your death in my place." God promises to accept all those who humbly come to him like this, looking to Christ as their deliverer. He will not and cannot turn any away who come to him pleading the precious name of Christ as their mediator.

This exchange deal is particularly good news to those of us who know that our goodness isn't nearly good enough. Some may fool themselves that God ought to be rather pleased with their righteousness. They think that they are doing quite nicely in obeying God and keeping his law. But others know the truth: we are miserable failures in our efforts to be good. We have not done what we ought or said what we ought or thought what we ought. As we look back over today and yesterday and last week, we lose count of the multitude of times we have failed God through lust, pride, selfishness, lies, coveting, and so on.

For people like us, the breastplate of God's righteousness is really good news. It declares that no matter how bad you've been, the offer of God's deliverance still stands. You can't pile more evil onto Jesus than he can bear! If he can carry the weight of the sins of all his people—past, present and future—then he can certainly manage your personal collection. That's why Christianity has long been good news to the outcasts of society. The gospel has always found a welcome among prostitutes and drug addicts, alcoholics and convicts, those enmeshed in sexual sin of various kinds, those who know they have lived immoral lives. All these can receive a perfect righteousness from Jesus Christ that makes them into the friends of God.

But the gospel is good news for the proud and the self-righteous as well. It is really hard work to maintain the facade of practical perfection, and to pretend to everyone around you that you really don't need a savior because you are doing just fine by yourself. It is a crushing burden to be the perfect elder brother in the parable of the Prodigal Son (see Luke 15:11–32), always staying home with Dad, doing what you should, while your heart secretly envies the apparent "freedom" of the younger brother. It wasn't love for his father but spiritual pride that led the elder brother to stay home. He was just as spiritually broken as his younger sibling; he was just better at hiding it. So, too, for many of us, it is actually our own weakness and the profound spiritual brokenness that lead us to behave so obediently. We don't actually obey God out of love and gratitude but out of a self-centered and joyless desire to prove our own value. In the gospel, elder brothers can also receive a new and perfect righteousness that is given to them as a free gift in Christ.

ASSURANCE AND CHALLENGE

This central truth of the imputed righteousness of Christ needs to dominate the lives of all Christians. On the one hand, it means that nothing I can do could ever stop God loving me. If God loved me enough to give himself for me when I was his sworn enemy, he will certainly love me enough to forgive me now that I am his adopted child. The righteousness that comes through the cross gives us assurance and security in God's love. If I have been reconciled to God through Christ and am always clothed in his perfect righteousness, then even during the darkest nights of personal failure, when I slide right back into those sins that have the strongest grip on my heart, he will not cast me off.

This can be a hard lesson to grasp, especially if you grew up in a home where every failure was counted against you, and you were loved or rejected on the basis of your performance. But your heavenly Father is a father who always stands waiting at the roadside for the prodigal to come home, always impatient to run to meet you, always hastening to replace your filthy rags with party clothes, and always ready to slay the fattened calf for a grand celebration. He welcomes you home on the basis of Christ's goodness, not your own.

On the other hand, the righteousness that comes through the cross also means that I can never take my sin lightly and just shrug it off. I have been reconciled to God and made a new creature in Christ (2 Cor. 5:17). God is now at work in me by his Holy Spirit, remaking me into the image of Christ. His purpose is to make me part of a holy people, created for good works in Christ Jesus (Eph. 2:10). Why, then, would I act as if I am still part of the kingdom of darkness and plunge back into my former way of life among the prostitutes and the pigs as if nothing had happened? The righteousness of Christ, painfully won for us at the cross, motivates us to strive hard toward an obedience that fits the new nature God is working in us.

DEFENDING THE VITAL ORGANS

When you see that the righteousness obtained for us on the cross gives us profound security in God's love and powerful motivation against sin, you can see why Paul describes righteousness as our breastplate in our fight against the devil. Just as a breastplate defends a soldier's vital organs, so the righteousness of Christ protects us against two of the chief lies that the devil wants us to believe, which are that God doesn't really love us and that sin doesn't really matter.

First, the devil works tirelessly to persuade you that God doesn't really love you. Satan says, "How could God love you when you are such a mess?" He whispers, "Maybe if you were a better Christian, God would love you, but he must surely have a constant frown on his face toward you because of your repeated failure. You are never going to amount to anything other than a cosmic disappointment in God's eyes."

Some of us have earthly fathers who seem constantly disappointed with us. But the righteousness that God has established for us through the blood of Christ speaks to us a better word, a word of God's unmerited favor. It says, "Beloved child, you have been reconciled to God through Christ's death and resurrection. Your sin and failure have been taken away, nailed to the cross once and for all as part of the charges against Christ. You have been joined to Christ forever in his holy perfection. So now, even though you are weak and failing, the Father cannot look at you apart from the perfect righteousness of Christ, which constantly melts his heart with love for you." We know that is really true because the righteousness of God has been given to us in Christ. As we strap that righteousness on as our breastplate, it protects our heart against Satan's vicious lie that God cannot really find pleasure in us.

But Satan also says, "Well, then, sin doesn't really matter. If God loves you just as much when you are bad as when you are good, why not be bad? It is so much easier and more fun." Yet precisely because of the perfect righteousness that has been given us in Christ, we cannot just continue in evil. In Christ, God declares us now to be what he will ultimately make us through the work of his

Spirit: perfectly righteous. In 1 Corinthians 6, Paul lists some of the activities that will keep some from inheriting the kingdom of God: sexual immorality, idolatry, adultery, practicing homosexuality, theft, greed, drunkenness, reviling, swindling, and so on. Many of the Corinthians to whom he wrote had once followed lifestyles that belonged on that list. But, Paul says, "you were washed, you were sanctified, you were justified in the name of the Lord Jesus Christ and by the Spirit of our God" (1 Cor. 6:11). The justification we receive in Christ is merely the start of God's work in us. New creation is the beginning of our transformation, not the end. The end of the story is the fulfillment of God's plan from the beginning of time: to have a holy people for himself, completely free from sin. In the meantime, our struggle with sin is an important part of the story God is writing by the work of the Holy Spirit in our hearts.

Of course, your story is not just about you. It is part of the much larger conflict against the spiritual powers in the heavenly realms, a battle in which God demonstrates his supreme power through our great weakness, frustrating Satan at every turn in his inability to maintain his hold on such desperately broken and fallen creatures.

Imagine how endlessly disappointing it must be to Satan to see weak human beings, who have absolutely no power in themselves to stand against his wiles, nonetheless snatched away from him by the greater power of God in the gospel! Time after time God says to him, "No, this one is mine!" and snatches another frail sinner from his clutches.

A DAILY STRUGGLE

We are not at the end of that story yet. We still have a long way to go in our journey as soldiers engaged in a lifelong conflict with Satan. It is a daily battle to put on the breastplate of God's righteousness and to fight with all our might to imitate that pattern of righteousness in our own lives. Sometimes it may seem like a losing battle, as the Spirit turns us over to our own power to show us our desperate weakness and exposes our constant need of Christ's goodness. At those times, we see clearly that only Christ's righteousness can possibly save us. At other times, God enables us to stand firm through his strengthening so that the spiritual world can be astonished at the ridiculous sight of weak, fallen flesh and blood withstanding everything that the terrifying powers of this present darkness can throw at them. How could that be anything other than the astonishing power of God at work? It is the breastplate of Christ's righteousness at work defending us against Satan's most potent lies.

So be on guard against your natural tendency to substitute your own righteousness for that of Christ. Notice the self-exalting and self-condemning thoughts that flow through your heart, moment by moment. If, when you are doing well, your mind is full of yourself, it is a sign that you are unduly enamored with your own armor. If, when you are failing, you are cast down with overwhelming feelings of guilt and shame, your problem is the same. Refocus your attention again on the gospel. Surround yourself with older, wiser, battle-hardened companions who can help you when the fight grows most intense. Young enthusiastic soldiers full of zeal for the battle can be a great encouragement, but sometimes we need to sit with those who have felt the heat of the conflict before and can remind us who must win the battle on our behalf.

In one sense, the average person is actually right in seeing that righteousness should mark out the Christian. Righteousness should be prominent in every Christian's life, as the breastplate that protects him against Satan's fiery arrows. We *are* right with God, through perfect obedience. But it is not our own weak and failing righteousness that guards us, not even our ability to strap on God's breastplate well; rather, it is a perfect righteousness that comes from God, a righteousness given to us in Christ as part of the cosmic transfer deal by which our own guilt was laid on Jesus. It is this imputed righteousness that is worked out in us as the Holy Spirit renews our thinking and renews our living. In that way, we begin to live the lives we were created to live, made like God in true righteousness and holiness. By God's grace, put on the breastplate of imputed righteousness so that you too may be increasingly strengthened to stand against the devil's schemes, upheld by the Lord's mighty, omnipotent hand.

FOR FURTHER REFLECTION

1. Why is it important that the righteousness in the breastplate of righteousness is God's and not our own?

2. How do we receive God's righteousness?

3. What practical difference should the breastplate of God's righteousness make in your life?

4. Why is the breastplate of righteousness good news for both "big sinners" and "elder brothers"?

GOSPEL BOOTS

Isaiah 52:7–11; Ephesians 6:15

In our culture, shoes are a fashion statement. People enjoy them as a way to express their individuality, not merely to cover their feet. It wasn't that way in ancient times. Most didn't have any shoes; they went barefoot. As a result, travel was slow and difficult, especially if the terrain was rough. Generally, the people most likely to have shoes (apart from the wealthy) were soldiers and couriers, people whose lives and livelihoods depended on their ability to travel far and fast. I know something of the value of proper footwear from my youth. One of my enduring childhood memories is being dragged on Marine Corps–style route marches on the Scottish hills, over loose rocks and through bogs. Thirteen miles may not seem much to a grown-up equipped with proper walking boots, but it can be absolute torture to a child in ordinary dress shoes, the only shoes I owned in those days. My feet weren't equipped for walking, so I wasn't prepared for the kind of activities that holidays in the Duguid household required.

PREPARED TO FACE LIFE

The apostle Paul doesn't want that experience to befall us as Christians. He wants us to be prepared for the travails of life in this difficult world, "having put on the readiness given by the gospel of peace" (Eph. 6:15). If you are to be engaged in an armed conflict, you can't afford to go unshod; you need proper footwear. The Romans understood this, so they equipped their soldiers with sturdy studded boots. Yet the primary background of Paul's imagery here is not the typical Roman soldier; it is once again the Old Testament. In Isaiah 52:7 the prophet declares:

> How beautiful up on the mountains
>   are the feet of him who brings good news,
> who publishes peace, who brings good news of happiness,
>   who publishes salvation,
>   who says to Zion, "Your God reigns."

This is the only other passage in the Bible where feet, good news, and peace occur together.

This Old Testament background is important because it clarifies a potential ambiguity in Paul's words. When Paul speaks of feet shod with the readiness of the gospel of peace, does he mean the readiness *given* by the gospel of peace or the readiness to *spread the good news* that brings peace? Many translations and commentaries go for the former interpretation, which is plausible both grammatically and contextually. But if Paul is making a connection with the Isaiah 52 passage, then the readiness he has in mind is primarily the readiness to share the good news as heralds of the gospel. It is true that we ourselves need to hear the good news of peace that we are called to share with others. Yet heralds primarily need good shoes to enable them to travel far and fast to bring their message to those waiting to hear good news.

Isaiah presents the image of watchmen bursting into joyful song on the walls of Jerusalem. These watchmen who had long strained their eyes with fearful anticipation of an approaching enemy army now become heralds declaring good news of deliverance to the beleaguered citizens of Zion. Paul applies this same image to our privilege of sharing the gospel of peace with believers and unbelievers alike. He makes the same connection when he cites both the prophet Joel and Isaiah in Romans 10:

> For "everyone who calls on the name of the Lord will be saved." How then will they call on him in whom they have not believed? And how are they to believe in him of whom they have never heard? And how are they to hear without someone preaching? And how are they to preach unless they are sent? As it is written: "How beautiful are the feet of those who preach the good news!" (Rom. 10:13–15)

Notice at once how differently these passages present the task of evangelism from the way in which we often conceive it. We sometimes think of evangelism as a kind of spiritual, multilevel marketing program, in which it is our job to browbeat friends and relations into making a purchase that they never needed or wanted, and then, if at all possible, recruit them into doing the same thing to their friends and relations. No wonder we aren't enthused about the prospect! Heralds are vastly different from Tupperware salespeople though. They don't have a product that needs to be marketed; they have wonderful good news that needs to be trumpeted! People may or may not choose to listen to that announcement. Our task is simply to proclaim the good news of God's peace to broken and oppressed souls, wherever and whenever we encounter them.

THE TASK OF THE HERALD

The task of being a herald is simple and twofold: to get the message right and to get the message out. To begin with, we need to get the message right. In Isaiah's context, the good news of peace we have been commissioned to share could be broken down into three statements: (1) your God reigns; (2) he has redeemed Jerusalem and comforted his people; (3) the ends of the earth will see the salvation of our God. Our message is essentially the same.

First, we announce to people that our God—Yahweh, the God of the Bible—reigns. In Isaiah's context, that news was a much-needed reminder that the idols of the Babylonians did not reign. Marduk and Bel were empty entities; Nebo was an anorexic god who had no power to bless or curse. It is still good news of peace for us in our contemporary context that our God reigns. Even though we don't worship those ancient gods, we still attribute the power to bless or to curse to all manner of things in this world. We say to beauty, "You are my god," or to success, "I worship you." We attribute to money the ability to declare us a valuable person, or to broken relationships the power to unmask us as failures. We say to our idols, "So long as I have you, I have meaning and significance in my life. If I lose you, I lose everything."

None of those things—money, beauty, authority, success, relationships—has real power over us; they are every bit as empty as the Babylonian idols of Old Testament times. Yet we and the people around us treat them as if they had enormous significance. As a result, we all live much of our lives in miserable bondage to our idols, making the endless sacrifices that they demand of us while always striving in pursuit of their elusive smile. Our false gods are harsh taskmasters. They may reward some of us with their fickle blessings, only to ensnare us even more deeply in their power, while they reduce others to nervous wrecks who feel devalued by their curses on our failures and shortcomings.

UNMASKING THE IDOLS

So what are the idols who reign in your life? For me, they tend to be money and productivity. When unexpected bills mount up, I can feel the rising fear in my heart. My idol is declaring me a failure. When my health prevents me from doing as much as I am used to doing, I become irritable. My idol is cursing me, and I respond with fear and anxiety. Others may have different idols, or they may respond to the same idols differently. Some respond to their idol's curse with anger, lashing out at those around them. Others find themselves sucked into addictive patterns of behavior, whether with food or alcohol, or even seemingly positive things like exercise or cleaning, as a way to escape the bad feelings triggered by our idols' curses.

As Christians, we have good news for a world that lies in bondage to these idols. The gospel gives us peace by declaring our freedom from false gods. They do not reign; the Lord reigns! He is the only one whose verdict on your life matters. If the Lord declares you cursed, nothing else can remedy your lostness. But if the Lord says you are blessed, then you are certainly blessed. In Christ, God declares that his people are blessed indeed, with every spiritual blessing (see Ephesians 1). If you are trusting in

Christ, you have the smile of the Father's favor resting upon you forever and an eternal inheritance that you cannot lose.

That declaration has peace-giving power. Anyone who believes in Christ has been entrusted by the Father into the Son's strong grasp, from which nothing and no one can ever wrest you away. Beauty cannot give you that peace, nor money, nor success, nor health, nor relationships. They don't reign. They can easily be lost and with them all hope of their blessing. But the Lord reigns! Because that is true, you can know that whatever you have of those things, you have as a good gift from your Father. Whatever you lack of those things, you lack because a loving Father knows that it would be better for you not to have them right now. These things are not your identity. If you lose any or all of those blessings, you still have the one thing that really matters in this world if you have Christ. You therefore have the freedom to enjoy whatever measure of those good things God has given you, but you also have the freedom to live at peace without them, knowing that they don't define you and give you your sense of value. They are not your peace.

THE LORD COMFORTS HIS PEOPLE—AND THE NATIONS

The second thing we are to announce is that the Lord has redeemed Jerusalem and comforted his people. This speaks of the incredible grace that comes to us in the gospel. The gospel is not the pronouncement that God loves good people and that if you get your act together, he might just love you too. That would certainly not have been good news for Isaiah's audience.

Early in the book of Isaiah, Jerusalem was comprehensively condemned for the repeated failure of both leaders and citizens. They had hard hearts, blind eyes, and deaf ears, repeatedly ignoring the Lord's entreaties through his prophet. Isaiah was told that this hardness of heart would persist for generations until a terrible judgment would come upon God's people because of their lengthy record of sin and failure (see Isa. 6:9–13).

Judgment would have been a fit end to their story—Jerusalem as a city with no survivors, like a tree chopped down and its trunk burned by fire. But even in the midst of pending judgment, the Lord gives hints of hope. Like a temporary shelter in a farmer's field (Isa. 1:8), something will survive the destruction; the tree will be cut down and burned, but there will be a stump left behind from which a new sprout will grow (Isa. 11:1). After many chapters of searching judgment, God sends out his heralds with comforting words of peace (Isa. 40:1–11). In spite of Israel's repeated sin, the Lord will not let his people go. There is hope yet for Israel.

What is more, the heralds were instructed to declare that this good news was not just for Israel. It was not confined to those physically descended from Abraham. Since Israel was to receive a salvation they had not earned or merited, a salvation entirely from the Lord's grace and mercy, that same salvation could even come to their former oppressors. Isaiah anticipated a highway that would unite Assyria and Egypt with Israel in a triple alliance, in which those old enemies would be made into new friends (Isa. 19:23–25). We miss the force of that statement because for us, "Egypt" and "Assyria" are just names from old history books, but these were countries that had brutally persecuted God's people. It is as if the Lord were to declare salvation for Nazi Germany and Soviet Russia, for violent jihadis in the Middle East and communist oppressors in China. As Assyria and Egypt were reconciled to Israel's God, they would be brought near to the renewed Israel as well.

It is this unlikely transformation of rebels and spiritual misfits into a group of faithful friends of God and each other that Jesus Christ came to accomplish. As we sing in our Christmas carols, Jesus himself is the shoot from that cut-down stump of Jesse, in whom we find peace with God. He is the true and faithful Israel who did what historical Israel never could—keeping God's law perfectly and thereby becoming a light to his own people, the descendants of Abraham after the flesh, and to the Gentiles as well (Isa. 49:6). According to Paul, Jesus entered this world to proclaim the good news of peace to those who were far away and peace to those who were near; that is, he came to bring Jews and Gentiles together in one new body through faith in Christ, through the work of the Spirit (Eph. 2:11–22).

JESUS CHRIST, OUR HERALD

These gospel sandals are yet another piece of the armor of God that Jesus wore first, in our place. Jesus came not merely as herald of the good news of our salvation but as its accomplisher. He laid down his own life for our sins so that we who were God's natural enemies could become his friends through simple faith in Christ. Through his death and resurrection, we have peace with God. As Jesus announced in his very first sermon, he is the Spirit-filled servant of the Lord from Isaiah 61 whom the Lord had anointed to proclaim good news to the poor; to heal the brokenhearted; to proclaim liberty to the captive and freedom to the prisoners; to proclaim the year of the Lord's favor; to comfort all who mourn; to provide for those who mourn in Zion; to give them a crown of beauty instead of ashes, festive oil instead of mourning, and splendid clothes instead of despair (see Luke 4:18–19).

Jesus is the perfect evangelist who never missed an opportunity to declare the good news of his own coming to a lost and needy world. He spoke about this salvation to the woman of Samaria who was an outcast to her own people, coming to the well to draw water during the heat of the day to cloak her shame over her five failed marriages (John 4:1–26). Jesus brought that good news of peace to lepers, bringing them healing and wholeness (Luke 5:12–13). His touch overpowered their disease, which emblemized the way in which sin eats away at whatever is whole and good until there is nothing left but a dead husk. Jesus even raised the dead, demonstrating his power over the last enemy (Mark 5:22–42). In doing these things, Jesus himself became our peace.

This peace was dramatically purchased through Jesus's death on the cross. There God treated the innocent One as guilty so that he could treat us, the guilty ones, as innocent. That is the very heartbeat of the gospel of peace. Now, because of what Jesus has done, we have an unshakable peace with God. We are no longer guilty in God's sight; that poisonous pile of our personal sins has been removed from our record and chalked up onto Jesus's record. Through his death and resurrection, we are now God's friends, part of God's family. We are no longer rebels on the run from an angry deity but beloved children with a safe, eternal home in heaven.

RECEIVING AND PROCLAIMING GOOD NEWS

Who needs to hear this good news? We ourselves are the first people who need to hear this good news of peace. We often don't have the unshakable peace that the gospel should bring us. We are undone by our own failures, as well as by the curses of our idols, which we continue to permit to define our lives. We need to hear the news that our God reigns and that he has provided us with the profound cleansing that makes us right with him. When we lack peace as believers, it is often because our eyes are fixed on ourselves and our own performance, as if that were the determining factor in our destiny. The remedy is to shift our eyes away from ourselves to our God and what he has done to cleanse us from our sin.

Isaiah had experienced that himself. When Isaiah first saw the Lord, he felt profoundly condemned by his own sinfulness (see Isa. 6:1–7). He knew he was a man whose lips were unclean, surrounded by a people similarly afflicted. How could such a person survive an encounter with the all holy, majestic God of glory? But the Lord sent an angel to touch his lips with a burning coal. We would expect that fiery touch to silence his unclean lips forever! Instead, astonishingly, it cleansed him of his iniquity. The coal came from the altar, the place of sacrifice, and pointed forward to the peace that God would ultimately establish through the cross. The prophet thus received the personal experience of redemption and hope that he was called to declare to others. As a result, when the Lord said, "Whom shall we send, and who will go for us?" (v. 8), Isaiah immediately knew the answer. Because of the cleansing he had received, Isaiah was prepared to endure faithfully in the hard ministry of declaring the news of God's reign to a people who, for the most part, wanted nothing to do with it. He was shod with gospel preparedness that carried him safely over the tough terrain that faced him.

The gospel of peace likewise gives us persistence in declaring the good news in the face of the difficulties and challenges of life. We have been made right with God. We have a glorious inheritance stored up with Christ. God has planned a wonderful future for us in a place where there is no more death, no more pain, no more frustration, no more tears. This present warfare is not all there is; our successes and failures do not define our existence. This struggle against Satan and his forces will not last forever. This route march will have an end; there will come a time for slipping off these boots and easing our weary feet into a nice, hot bath.

PEACE FOR THE HERALDS

The gospel of peace enables us to rest, even when we fail in sharing the good news. Most of us are not great evangelists. We forget the good news of peace on a daily basis and are often terrified by the prospect of telling others about Jesus. Some of us feel very guilty about our lack of evangelistic zeal. We fear that God must be disappointed with us because we don't spend every waking moment deliberately active in proclaiming the gospel news. As a result, we become spiritual workaholics, driven by our secret fear so that we harass everyone around us with the name of Jesus, or we give up altogether on evangelism, convincing ourselves that it is too hard for anyone other than experts.

But even while the gospel of peace stirs up our hearts to make us want to share that good news, it also gives us peace in those times when we are unable or unwilling to shout out the gospel. It reminds us that our God reigns in evangelism, as he does in everything else. No one will be eternally lost because of your failures or mine—God doesn't give us that power. God created the universe out of nothing; he raises up empires and crushes them with a snap of his fingers. He is certainly *not* holding his breath to see if you or I will obey him and share the good news so that his plans for world redemption won't be shipwrecked.

Jesus himself is still the primary herald of the good news. When we quote the great commission—"Go therefore and make disciples of all nations, baptizing them in the name of the Father and of the Son and of the Holy Spirit, teaching them to observe all that I have commanded you"—we often seem to forget the last part: "and behold, I am with you always, to the end of the age" (Matt. 28:19–20). Jesus is with us by his Spirit, opening our dumb mouths to speak and preparing open ears to hear and soft hearts to receive his truth. He is still bringing good news to the Gentiles and shining a great light on those who dwell in deep darkness. On that last day, not one of his flock will be missing; every single sheep will be present and accounted for.

With that knowledge, we have both the boldness to speak and the security to rest. We have ourselves received cleansing from our sins and are authorized to tell others where they too can receive similar cleansing. As D. T. Niles famously said, "Evangelism is just one beggar telling another beggar where to find bread."[1] At the same time, we know that we are not personally responsible for the salvation of everyone around us. That is God's job, not ours.

Jesus persistently and faithfully spoke good news of peace to a motley crew of incompetent and often ungrateful disciples, as well as to an often unreceptive wider Jewish audience. He was never discouraged by those who rejected his message, because his ultimate desire was always to do his Father's will, not simply to get people to believe in him. He kept his eyes on the goal throughout the long race and thereby became the goal upon which we are to set our eyes during our own race. Was anyone ever less frantic and more at peace than Jesus? No one ever had more on

---

1. Daniel T. Niles, *That They May Have Life* (New York: Harper & Brothers, 1951), 96.

his to-do list than Jesus—preach the gospel, heal the sick, train the disciples, save the world. Yet in the midst of all that busyness he was at peace; he had time for people, time for life, and, most importantly, time to spend with God. He wasn't constantly trying to earn his Father's favor, so he could rest content with the good deeds his Father had placed in his path for that day. In contrast to our harried and hurried lives, Jesus shows us a life lived at God's pace—never lazy or idle but never driven either, calmly communicating the good news of his own presence to all those whom his Father brought across his path. He did that for us so that we too could have peace with God—a message of good news for ourselves and to share with all those around us.

FOR FURTHER REFLECTION

1. Why is it good news to be reminded that it is your God who reigns?

2. What idols contest the fact of God's reign in your life?

3. Who do you know who would benefit from God's peace? Make a list of three or four people with whom you would love to share this good news. Then ask God to create opportunities for that conversation.

4. How does Jesus give us peace in our own flawed efforts to reach out with the good news?

5

THE SHIELD OF FAITH

Ephesians 6:16

The vital importance of faith is a central theme in many movies. Is the protagonist going to believe and conquer, no matter how seemingly impossible the odds, or give in to doubt and fail? Inevitably, faith wins out: the lead character chooses to trust, and all ends well. But what exactly are we supposed to believe in? That part of the equation is often obscure. Is it faith in ourselves, faith in the power of teamwork, faith in our destiny, or something else? The object of your faith doesn't seem to matter too much in these movies; what matters is simply that you "keep the faith" and "don't stop believing."

As a result of this common cultural emphasis, people sometimes say, "I wish I could believe in Christianity, but I'm afraid I just can't believe that people rise from the dead. I think it is wonderful that you believe though. I'm glad for you that you have your faith." Such people do not understand the biblical concept of faith, however, which is rooted in reality. If there is no solid foundation to faith, then faith itself is worse than useless; it is false and misleading. I may firmly believe that I could yet have a future in professional rugby as a skinny, not particularly fast fifty-six-year-old, but frankly that is never going to happen, nor was it even when I was fifteen.

In biblical terms, faith must always have a firm foundation if it is to be meaningful, or it is simply a glorious falsehood. Faith is not, as the skeptic Ambrose Bierce once defined it, "belief without evidence in what is told by one who speaks without knowledge of things without parallel."[1] That is why Paul told the Corinthians, "If in Christ we have hope in this life only, we are of all people most to be pitied" (1 Cor. 15:19). If Jesus Christ's resurrection is a myth or a fantasy, it is not a charming delusion to be tolerated or encouraged because it enables some people to live happier and more moral lives. Faith in the resurrection is only meaningful if it is actually true. True biblical faith derives its power not from any power inherent in faith itself but rather from the object of that faith. Faith is merely the instrument that connects us to the utterly trustworthy and all-powerful God, who created the heavens and the earth and who made us for relationship with him.

This is the faith of which Paul is speaking in our passage when he says, "In all circumstances take up the shield of faith, with which you can extinguish all the flaming darts of the evil one" (Eph. 6:16). He is not saying that faith has some remarkable defensive power against Satan, in and of itself. Rather, he is saying that faith protects us from Satan's attacks because of

---

1. Ambrose Bierce, *The Devil's Dictionary* (New York: Sagamore Press, 1957).

what faith enables us to take hold of, namely, the power and protection of God himself.

GOD IS OUR SHIELD

This becomes clear when you look at the usage of shield imagery in the Old Testament. Throughout the Old Testament it is not faith but God who is repeatedly described as our shield. In Genesis 15:1 the Lord tells Abraham, "I am your shield; your reward shall be very great." Proverbs 30:5 says: "[God] is a shield to those who take refuge in him." This same theme is repeated many times in the psalms. For example, in Psalm 3:3 David says: "You, O LORD, are a shield about me, my glory, and the lifter of my head." In Psalm 28:7 we read, "The LORD is my strength and my shield." In Psalm 119:114 the psalmist says to the Lord, "You are my hiding place and my shield."

Perhaps the closest parallel to our passage in Ephesians 6, however, is Psalm 91. This psalm deals with a believer who finds himself under attack from warfare, plague, pestilence, and the arrows of his enemies. Many commentators have discerned a spiritual dimension to the assaults described in this psalm. The psalmist affirms that in the midst of that all-encompassing assault, he will be safe:

> He will deliver you from the snare of the fowler
>> and from the deadly pestilence.
> He will cover you with his pinions,
>> and under his wings you will find refuge;
>> his faithfulness is a shield and buckler.
> You will not fear the terror of the night,
>> nor the arrow that flies by day,

> nor the pestilence that stalks in darkness,
>> nor the destruction that wastes at noonday. (Ps. 91:3–6)

God himself is our shield; he is our refuge; he is our hiding place in the day of difficulty; his faithfulness will keep us safe when we are being shot at by arrows, flaming or otherwise.

THE SHIELD OF FAITH

But if the Old Testament tells us that God is our shield, why does Paul say that faith is our shield? Faith is the means by which we flee to God for refuge. It is how we cling to God and find in him comfort and protection in times of difficulty and distress. Imagine you have fallen into the sea and are drowning. You can't swim, and there is nothing you can do to save yourself. But then somebody throws you a rope. If you grab hold of that rope, you can be pulled to safety, but in order to be saved, several things are necessary. First, you need to believe in the existence of the rope and that there is someone at the other end of it. If there is no rope, there is nothing to grab. If there is no one at the other end of the rope, there would equally be no point in grabbing it.

But it's not enough to believe in the existence of the rope and of someone at the other end of the rope; you also need to be convinced the person at the other end of the rope wants to help you. If it were wartime, and the person at the other end of the rope were an enemy, there might be no point in grabbing the rope, because the enemy might shoot you anyway. But if the person on the other end of the rope were your best friend, you would confidently grab the rope. Yet you could believe all these things and still drown if you didn't actually grab the rope. If all your beliefs don't lead you to the necessary action, then they won't do you any good.

This picture helps us understand what Christians mean when they talk about faith. Faith is not simply saying, "I believe in God." Such a generic belief in a supreme being is not what Paul means. He is talking about faith in the specific God who loved the world so much that he gave his only Son so that we should not perish but have everlasting life. Yet even when we are able to define faith in biblical terms, we might have to confess that our faith isn't the shield it should be against the flaming arrows of the enemy. Our beliefs aren't always a consoling and sustaining reality in the midst of the greatest stresses and trials of life. Maybe you are bent over in the midst of a spiritual or emotional hurricane, and your faith is *not* acting as a shield for you right now. At the time you most need it, you feel unable to take up the shield of faith and use it as God intended.

Why isn't your faith a shield for you in the midst of the storm? Well, to throw you back into the sea for a moment, the simple belief that there is somebody at the other end of the rope is not enough. It is not enough to believe that there is a God somewhere out there. You have to know he has the power to deliver you—to pull you in, if you like. For faith to be your shield, you need to believe that God is sovereign over every detail of the universe. You must know that your God directs not only the affairs of men and nations but ordains the car crash, the job layoff, the health challenges, the relational difficulties. Each of these things comes into our life because God, the supreme commander of the universe, has dictated it to be so. This is where our functional unbelief is so often a problem. We may confess in theory the doctrine of God's sovereignty, but we have a hard time holding on to that truth in the desperately difficult challenges of life in a fallen world, where the powers of evil around us often seem very strong, and our world seems totally out of control.

To experience faith as a shield, you need to know not only that God is powerful but that this God is your friend. God's sovereignty is not in the least comforting unless you know that this sovereign God is on your side. Here, too, we often struggle. In the midst of the intense pain of life, we find it hard to believe that God is really on our side. Perhaps you have prayed to God desperately and nothing has happened. The doubts easily creep in. Your belief in God won't shield you if you don't believe God is *for* you.

FAITH BUILT ON TRUTH

That is why it is so important we build our faith on the truth, God's Word. Our feelings about whether God exists and who he is rise and fall like the tides, but God's truth in the Bible endures forever. What is the Bible's answer to the question about whether God is on our side? Strangely enough, it starts out by recognizing that God isn't automatically on everybody's side. God is not a great grandfather in the sky who exists to make every human life happy and fulfilled. In chapter 2, Paul told the Ephesians about their natural state before they became Christians. He said to them in essence, "You were dead in your transgressions and your sins. You were by nature objects of God's wrath. God wasn't on your side, because you were his enemy and he was yours. You were drowning, and you had no claim on God. There was no reason for him to throw you the rope, because you spent all your time rebelling against him and the things he told you to do." That is true not just of the Ephesians but of all of us. We are all by nature utterly lost.

Some people have a hard time accepting that fact. They say, "Wait a minute. I wasn't God's enemy. I believed in his existence. I tried to be a good person. I even went to church sometimes." The problem is that you just don't see how radical God's claims on your life are. The first commandment that God gave to Israel was, "You shall have no other gods before me" (Ex. 20:3). In other words God says, "Nothing is to be more precious to you than me." Now, which of us can truly say that we've kept that commandment? We can't even keep the commandments that tell us to honor our parents (v. 12), not to kill (v. 13), not to commit adultery (v. 14), not to steal (v. 15), and not to covet (v. 17)!

That is especially true when we remember that it is not just our actions that count against us but even our thought life (see Matthew 5:21–28). Which of us has never been envious of something somebody else has, or lusted after someone, or been sinfully angry? What is more—we've never had to work at learning how to do wrong. I remember teaching my children many things—how to tie their shoes, how to wipe their noses, how to say please and thank you—but I never said, "Now, this is how to sin." That came naturally to them, as it does to me. By nature, we were born God's enemies. We were drowning in our rebellion, and God had absolutely no reason to rescue us.

But he did. That is the amazing message of Christianity. God was our enemy, and there wasn't a single thing we could do about it. We didn't even want to do anything about it. But God, who is rich in mercy, made us alive in Christ (Eph. 2:4). He didn't wait for us to start swimming in the right direction; in Christ, God himself swam out to us in order to demonstrate beyond a shadow of a doubt that he is on our side. He did that through the great exchange of the gospel: God the Father treated Jesus, the only innocent person who ever lived, as if he were guilty so that he could treat us, the guilty, as though we were innocent. The Father poured out all his anger and wrath against sin upon the Son. There on the cross, Jesus suffered the physical and mental and spiritual anguish that our many sins deserved, along with the many sins of all his people. The cross reached back into history and paid for the sins of God's Old Testament people, and it reaches forward to the end of history and pays for all God's New Testament people as well. If you are a Christian today, then the cross has paid for all your sins—past, present, and future. Now you are God's friend. You have been reconciled to God, so you can feel confident that when he brings you the rope, he will also pull you in. What counts is not the strength of your faith, let alone the strength of your faithfulness. Your security lies in the fact that Jesus has been faithful for you; his strength, as the One in whom our faith rests, is our sure and certain hope.

FAITH POINTS TO GOD'S PROMISES

When the flaming darts of the evil one are flying, how can faith guard and strengthen you in your spiritual war against Satan? First, faith points our eyes toward the *promises of God*. Faith, says the writer to the Hebrews, is being sure of what we hope for and certain of what we don't see (Heb. 11:1). Faith reminds us that this war is not all there is. God has promised us a wonderful future in his presence. We have a glorious inheritance stored up in Christ in comparison to which our present difficulties will seem like light and momentary afflictions. The end of the journey is just around the corner.

By faith, I lay hold of that truth by reminding myself of the promises of God. God has promised to be with me when I walk through deep and desperate trials (Ps. 23:4). He has assured me that all things must work together for good for those who love him and are called according to his purpose (Rom. 8:38). I know these things because God has promised them to me in his Word. He's proved himself faithful, so even though I don't know how the future will work out, I know he holds it in his hands. I don't know what terrible things I may do, or the sins that others around me may commit against me, but I do know that God is sovereign even over these things. Faith reminds me, "God has promised to work this situation out, and I believe he will because we've been reconciled through the cross. Having loved me that much, he won't abandon me now. He will not bring one iota of pain into my life that isn't absolutely necessary for my growth and sanctification."

Faith helps us as it lays hold of the promises of God in the darkest of days. When the evil one throws his flaming darts at you that say, "God doesn't really care about you, or this bad thing wouldn't be happening," faith puts out the fire. Just as when parents take a young child for an injection, as the needle approaches, she clings tighter and tighter to them, and she doesn't understand. So also when the needles of life are getting awfully close, by faith we lean in and cling tighter to the God who we know loves us, even when we cannot understand.

FAITH LAYS HOLD OF GOD'S POWER

When the evil one tempts you by saying: "You can't help yourself. You know you are going to give in to this temptation eventually, because I'm stronger than you," faith puts out the fire. Faith recalls what God's Word says: "He who is in you is greater than he who is in the world" (1 John 4:4). I can't take on Satan, but God can. In the midst of temptation, by faith we lean in to our

Father's greater strength. When we find ourselves in confusing circumstances, faith points us to our Father's wisdom. Maybe I don't know what to say to a particular person, but God knows what he needs. Perhaps I cannot see any possible way forward in troubling circumstances, but God knows the future, and by faith I trust that at the right moment, things will become clear. By faith we lean into our Father's greater wisdom.

Indeed, whenever we pray by faith, we are leaning into the power and wisdom of God. Prayer is not a trick whereby we get God to do our bidding and command him to order the universe according to our wisdom. When we pray, we bring our cares and requests to God, confident in his great power and love for us, knowing that he will do whatever is best for us. That confidence in the great power of God and of his love for us is the essence of faith. When we pray, we are confessing that God is on our side. We are acknowledging that God has great power and wisdom for every circumstance. And we believe these things not because of some fantasy of wishful thinking but because we see them conclusively demonstrated in the death and resurrection of Jesus Christ. In Christ's death, we see the love of God that will not let us go, sinners and rebels though we are. In Christ's resurrection, we see the power of God displayed, a power that can destroy sin once and for all without destroying the sinner. Through his resurrection, Christ commits himself to accomplish that same eternal, holy, and pure life in me on the day of his appearing.

HELP MY UNBELIEF!

There is one more thing to say: even when I don't believe with my whole heart that God is sovereign and good, which is often, that doesn't change the truth. Our constant cry is, "I believe; Lord, help my unbelief!" And he does. Remember, it is not ultimately our faith that shields us but God himself. When the shield of our faith wavers and drops, the Lord's strong and mighty shield is always in place, keeping us safe from Satan's assaults. In Luke 22:31–32 Jesus said to Peter, "Satan demanded to have you, that he might sift you like wheat, but I have prayed for you that your faith may not fail." Strikingly, the first "you" is plural in Greek. Satan wants to sift all of us like wheat and, just as he did with Peter, God may allow that to happen. He may allow the utter weakness of our faith to be exposed by our inability to head off those darts of Satan, just as was the case for Peter and the first disciples. Jesus didn't pray that Peter wouldn't get sifted by Satan; he prayed that when he was sifted, his faith wouldn't fail. So too Jesus, your great High Priest, prays for you, that in the midst of your trials and many failures, your faith would not fail. Here is good news indeed, for Jesus's prayers are always answered.

Faith is a shield as it connects us to the fundamental realities of the promises of God in the gospel. By faith, trust in the goodness of God demonstrated in the death of Jesus Christ to get you into heaven. By faith, grab the rope that God has put before you, confident that God himself will bring you safely home. By faith, trust in the power of God, the same power that raised Jesus Christ from the dead and seated him at the right hand of God. By faith, believe in God's unshakable love toward you in Christ, a love that will never let you go. As you trust in the goodness, power, and love of God, you have a shield that will put out the flaming arrows of the evil one. Even more importantly, in God's faithfulness you have a shield that will certainly keep you safe, weak though your own faith may be, until the day you pass through the gates of death into life that will last forever.

FOR FURTHER REFLECTION

1. Give an example of a recent situation in which your faith in God was a powerful shield for you.

2. Why is it important that your faith be built on truth?

3. Where does your faith most struggle: to believe either in God's power, or his love, or his personal interest in you?

4. List some Bible verses that help strengthen your faith that God is for you.

5. How do Jesus's death and resurrection encourage your faith?

6

THE HELMET OF SALVATION

Ephesians 6:17

In the unlikely case that we forget to put on our shoes before leaving the house, one step on gravel soon reminds us. Other necessities aren't so quickly remembered—an umbrella, for example. I have left several umbrellas on buses, never missing them until the first drops of rain hit. By then it is too late, and you get soaked. Is a soldier's helmet more like shoes, which are hard to forget, or like an umbrella, which is hard to remember? Clearly, a helmet could be an easily forgotten item, because until a crisis hits and the bullets begin to fly, a soldier doesn't really feel the need for it. When life gets hard, you find out what your headgear is made of. Is it a helmet or a floppy hat that may keep the sun out of your eyes but won't divert a sword blade?

RIGHTEOUSNESS AND SALVATION

Paul calls the Christian's headgear the "helmet of salvation," an image that, like the breastplate of righteousness, is borrowed directly from the description of the divine warrior in Isaiah 59:17. In fact, God's righteousness and his people's salvation occur together frequently in the book of Isaiah. They have a cause-and-effect relationship. God's righteousness—his reliable commitment to fulfill all his promises to his people—means that he must act to deliver them from all their enemies. This includes not merely their physical enemies, such as the Assyrians and Babylonians, but the greatest enemy of all—their sin—and the separation from God that that sin causes. In Isaiah 51, the Lord declares:

> My righteousness draws near,
>> my salvation has gone out,
>> and my arms will judge the peoples;
> the coastlands hope for me,
>> and for my arm they wait.
> Lift up your eyes to the heavens,
>> and look at the earth beneath;
> for the heavens vanish like smoke,
>> the earth will wear out like a garment,
>> and they who dwell in it will die in like manner;
> but my salvation will be forever,
>> and my righteousness will never be dismayed.
>
> Listen to me, you who know righteousness,
>> the people in whose heart is my law;
> fear not the reproach of man,
>> nor be dismayed at their revilings.
> For the moth will eat them up like a garment,
>> and the worm will eat them like wool;
> but my righteousness will be forever,
>> and my salvation to all generations. (vv. 5–8)

Because of God's righteousness, Israel's ultimate salvation was assured. In the midst of the very real trials of the Babylonian exile and the resulting doubts about whether the Lord had abandoned them because of their sins, God's people could be encouraged by the confident hope that God's promises would not fail. People come and go; empires rise and fall; even the earth and the heavens themselves will one day wear out like an old garment, disappearing like the smoke that rises from a smoldering fire. But because the Lord is righteous, he must and will fulfill everything that he has promised, including the deliverance and restoration of his people. This firm promise of God provides the basis for their secure hope in the midst of life's trials and difficulties, that God will save and deliver his people in the end. That is why, in 1 Thessalonians 5:8, Paul describes this piece of armor more fully as "*the hope of* salvation." The Christian's helmet is his or her sure hope of salvation.

THE HOPE OF SALVATION

At this point we need to be clear what we mean by the hope of salvation. Most people are hoping to be saved. Nobody wants to go to hell, and not many people actually think that they will. But that is not what Paul means by the hope of salvation; in terms of battle headgear, that kind of "hoping to be saved" is as much use as a floppy sun hat. It may feel comfortable, but it is not going to do you much good when the conflict grows fierce. In the Bible, hope is never a vague optimism that everything is going to work out in the end. Rather, hope is a settled conviction about where one will spend eternity. Biblical hope is sufficiently sure that you can give a reason for it (see 1 Pet. 3:15). Yet many people can't give a good reason for their vague feeling that they are going to heaven.

One evangelistic outreach program suggests asking people, "If you were to die tonight and God were to ask you, 'Why should I let you into my heaven?' what would you say?" That's a great diagnostic question, but one for which many don't have an answer. They can think of no clear reason why God should let them into heaven. Others reply, "I've tried my best to obey the Ten Commandments and to love others as I love myself; I think overall I'm probably no worse than anyone else." These people have a reason for their hope but a very uncertain reason. If you are depending on your own goodness to get you into heaven, then you could never know for sure that is where you are going. How good is good enough to meet God's standard? What if you do something dreadful later on in life? When I look into my own heart and see all the wrong things I think and do every single day, I know that I, for one, don't have any chance of going to heaven based on my record. Certainly I could never be *sure* of going to heaven on my own goodness.

But the Bible tells us we can know for sure that we are going to heaven. The apostle John says, "I write these things to you who believe in the name of the Son of God, that you may know that you have eternal life" (1 John 5:13). John wants us to know for sure that we are going to heaven. How could we know such a thing for sure? Certainly we can't if it depends on our own goodness. But John explains how we can know this when he says, "This is the testimony, that God gave us eternal life, and this life is in his Son. Whoever has the Son has life; whoever does not have the Son of God does not have life" (1 John 5:11–12). John explains it in simple terms. If we have Jesus, we have life. If we don't have Jesus, we don't have life. Eternal life is God's free gift, which comes to us wrapped up in his Son. We receive Jesus Christ, and along with him we receive life. Turn our back on Jesus, and in the very same motion we are turning our back on heaven.

If you can understand that, then you understand why Christians can be sure about going to heaven. If attaining heaven depends on our best efforts, it must always remain uncertain. But if heaven is simply received as a free gift, then we can know that we have it for sure. As surely as we have received Jesus's perfect goodness and asked for all our rottenness to be laid on him, so surely we have received heaven. Dressed in the breastplate of his righteousness, given to us as a free gift of grace, we can be utterly confident of our eternal future. God's righteousness and the firm hope of salvation belong together in our lives, just as they do in the book of Isaiah.

CONFIDENT ASSURANCE

That's why there is nothing arrogant about saying that we know for sure we are going to heaven. Indeed, we would be incredibly prideful to rest our hope of heaven in our own goodness. But if our salvation is a free gift that comes to us by simple faith in Christ, then there is nothing arrogant in claiming such knowledge. We are simply taking God at his Word. After all, if God has given our salvation to us, who can snatch it away? Imagine that you are a small boy who has been given a beautiful, brand-new mountain bike. Would you be confident riding it around on your own in a rough neighborhood? You might be afraid that someone bigger than you would come along and steal it. But suppose you were there with your dad, who just happens to be six feet four and 300 pounds of muscle, a former college boxer. Who's going to bother you then? Who are you going to be afraid of? No one in their right mind would tangle with your dad.

We can even go further. As we said in earlier chapters, we are able to wear the armor of God with confidence because Jesus wore it first for us. In Isaiah 59:17 it was the Lord himself who donned righteousness as his breastplate and put the helmet of salvation on his head. This means that Jesus not only lived a spotless life of perfect righteousness in our place; he also hoped perfectly in our place. Jesus knows what it is to endure trials and suffering, while keeping his hope in the Father's care intact. Whereas I am often frantic and fearful in difficult circumstances, easily forgetting my hope, the book of Hebrews tells us that Jesus "learned obedience through what he suffered" (5:8). "For the joy that was set before him [Jesus] endured the cross, despising the shame" (12:2). Jesus's hope has already been vindicated; he is now seated at the right hand of the Father (12:2) and has become the source of eternal salvation for all those who obey him (5:9). The head that once was crowned with thorns is now wreathed in eternal glory. Because Jesus has worn the armor of God first, accomplishing perfect righteousness through his spotless life and winning our salvation through his atoning death, we are able now confidently to wear the helmet of the hope of salvation. Our salvation has already been accomplished for us by Christ; all that waits is the full harvest of that salvation.

PROTECTION AND BOLDNESS

That kind of solid hope is a practical kind of helmet. Helmets provide the soldier with protection against bullets and blows; in a similar way, the hope of salvation provides a real protection for the Christian in times of difficulty or distress. It defends the Christian against discouragement and despair. Why should you be discouraged by your present challenging circumstances when you have such a glorious and secure inheritance awaiting you? Suppose tomorrow you received two letters. In one, you received the news that your great-auntie Freda in Australia had died and left you ten million dollars, while in the same post you also received a parking ticket that was going to cost you fifty dollars. Which of the two letters is going to shape your day—the sure and certain hope of ten million dollars or the present depressing reality of the fifty-dollar fine?

If you are anything like me, there are plenty of times when the present fifty-dollar crisis easily wins out. Today's "momentary light affliction," as Paul describes it in 2 Corinthians 4:17, doesn't *feel* light and momentary; such afflictions often feel like life-shaping, soul-crushing burdens that seem impossible to bear. But in the light of the certain hope of our salvation, these burdens are put in a larger perspective. We know that God is up to something good in our life through our afflictions, producing perseverance and character. God tells us, "Count it all joy, my brothers, when you meet trials of various kinds, for you know that the testing of your faith produces steadfastness" (James 1:2–3). Yet if it is just for present benefits that we suffer, trials can be discouraging. Trials don't always bring immediate fruit in terms of measurable changes in our character. We often seem to go round and round in circles, sinning in precisely the same ways as so often before, failing to grow in the least in endurance and faith. Hope encourages us by reminding us of the greater realities yet to come. On the day of Christ Jesus, God will bring to completion the good work he has begun in us (Phil. 1:6). He has promised it, and he is faithful, even when we are not.

Doubt about your eternal salvation naturally leads on a trajectory that ends in despair: if you doubt God's desire and ability to save you ultimately, why should you believe in his desire and ability to watch over you in the present storms of life? But hope supports you in your deepest afflictions. Hope protects you when you are sick and when you are sad; hope sustains you when you are rejected and when you are lonely; hope bears you up when you are depressed and downcast; and hope strengthens you even when you stare face-to-face at the last enemy—death itself. Death shall not have the final victory. The Christ in whom your hope rests has already triumphed; he has risen from the dead and ascended into glory! If Jesus has already defeated death and purchased your place in heaven, why would he not also be triumphant over all the lesser trials and difficulties that you face in your life? If even death cannot separate you from the love of God in Jesus Christ, then certainly sickness, failure, abuse, broken relationships, financial difficulties, ongoing struggles with sin and fear, and anything else in all creation surely cannot!

Your hope of salvation thus protects you in the deepest, darkest valleys of your life by reminding you of God's power and his care for you. Of course, hope encourages you to hold lightly to the good things of this world as well, for these too we shall also leave behind one day. The highs as well as the lows in life are put in their proper perspective in the light of the all-surpassing glory of our salvation in Jesus Christ.

What is more, as a helmet, hope gives you boldness in faithfully pursuing God's call on your life. Sometimes God calls us to do risky things for him; at other times, faithfulness looks like persisting in doing ordinary things over and over again, trusting that the Lord will bring fruit we cannot yet see. The hope of salvation encourages us in both areas. If God calls us to risky obedience, hope reminds us that we are safe in his hands. God is sovereign over all the challenges and dangers we may ever be called to face. And if God calls us to serve faithfully in an area where there is little visible fruit for our efforts, hope reminds us that what we see is not what we get. If God has loved us enough to send Christ to the cross on our behalf, he will not waste a life lived in faithfulness to his call.

Certainly he doesn't promise to glorify us in all of our efforts to serve him. Our attempts may indeed end in failure from a human perspective, even when we are genuinely pursuing his leading. We may fail in our marriages, in our parenting, in our careers, and in our ministering, whether through adverse circumstances or our own sin. Yet even in that apparent failure, the Lord promises to glorify himself in and through us. Our labor in Christ cannot and will not ultimately be in vain, even if the only visible fruit is a single human life—ours—growing in gratitude to the God who called us and sustains us by his grace. What a tremendous encouragement that is to us to step out boldly in faith for him, trusting him to supply all our needs in Christ Jesus!

Hope also encourages us to resist sin, knowing that one day sin will be left behind. God's promise is this: sin shall not have dominion over us (Rom. 6:14). In this life we may struggle and fail repeatedly with besetting sins. That is why such sin is called "besetting." The fight for sanctification often feels like what happened in the movie *Groundhog Day*, in which Bill Murray's character was forced to live the same day over and over again. That is the normal way in which God teaches us the depth of our brokenness and our utter inability to change through our own willpower, so that we come to treasure the beauty of the gospel more deeply. But however many times we struggle against sin and fail in this life, our failure is not the last word; the last word is Christ's perfection, which clothes us, and the ongoing work of the Holy Spirit within us. God has promised that he will ultimately present us to himself perfect in Christ, and he will do just that! Hope gives us a holy patience to endure the present struggle alongside a holy impatience with our present weaknesses, as we long increasingly to be done with what Paul calls "this body of death" (Rom. 7:24) and to be renewed fully in holiness and purity.

PUTTING ON THE HELMET

Many people would be glad to escape from going to hell, but they are quite happy to settle for the best that this world can give. If they could make some money, have some friends and a family, and find a measure of satisfaction, that would be enough for them. Their best life now is all they seek. As Christians, though, we have a hope that one day we are going to live in God's presence forever. We are going to be made perfect, fit to live before him. What a glorious prospect! I long to get rid of my weaknesses, my sinfulness, my lack of love for others, my pride, my half-heartedness! I know it will happen one day, and I want that day to be soon.

Do you share that feeling? That should motivate you to strive hard to live that kind of life now. Pursue your hope with a passion! Try your best to be as holy in your living now as you say you hope to be in heaven. Put aside the things that hold you back—your earthly ambitions and desires, your pet sins, the things that weigh more heavily on your mind than God—and press on toward the goal. Live up to your hope! But always remember that the heartbeat of your hope lies not in the success of your present pursuit of holiness but in the sovereign and perfect work of God. The pace and progress of that work lie in his hands, not yours.

How can we stir up the embers of our hope so that it becomes a burning and vital force in our lives? The key surely lies in remembering and thinking often about the glories of our salvation. If you have forgotten about the ten-million-dollar inheritance by the time the parking ticket hits, your hope cannot do anything to protect you. But if you spend every moment of the day thinking, planning, wondering, and visualizing your new life as a millionaire, the parking ticket is less likely to throw you into a downward spiral of despair.

This is what happens in other areas of our lives. Would-be brides spend all day leafing through *Southern Wedding* magazine, dreaming about exotic colors like cerise and mauve, imagining flower arrangements and musical selections. They don't even necessarily need a fiancé. All of this can be triggered sometimes just because a cute guy smiled at them on the train! How much more profoundly should our thoughts be shaped constantly by our hope of heaven? Study those passages of Scripture that talk about what heaven is going to be like. Read books and listen to sermons that flood your thinking with the gospel. Think about what it will be like to stand before God and enjoy his presence forever. Imagine him saying to you, and to those around you, those astonishing words, "Welcome, beloved child, for whom Christ died. Enter into your inheritance." Reflect on what that salvation cost each time you come to the Lord's Table—his body broken for your salvation, his blood shed as the foundation for the new covenant that undergirds your hope. Remind yourself of how much you have been forgiven, even today. Ponder the fact that Jesus is even now king: he reigns in heaven now and one day every knee shall bow before him. Remind yourself of these truths to stir your hope of salvation into life so that it colors and shapes your view of your present circumstances, giving you boldness in the midst of trials and confidence in the face of great opposition and personal weakness. Put on the helmet of the hope of your salvation: experience the joy and boldness that come from the certainty of your righteousness in Christ and the solid assurance that the one who began that good work in you will bring it to completion on the day of Christ Jesus.

FOR FURTHER REFLECTION

1. What is the foundation of your hope that God will welcome you into heaven?

2. Why should all Christians have assurance of their salvation? Why might real Christians nonetheless struggle with assurance?

3. How does your hope of heaven encourage you in the midst of trials? Give a recent example where this happened (or perhaps where it should have but didn't).

4. In what area of your life do you need the boldness that hope gives?

5. Why is it good news for you that Jesus has hoped perfectly?

7

THE SWORD OF THE SPIRIT

Isaiah 49:2; Ephesians 6:17

Warfare has changed a great deal over the past two thousand years. Nowadays, much of it is done with clinical efficiency at a safe distance. There are laser-guided smart bombs, cruise missiles, and drones. In some ways, the modern soldier can simply light the fuse and stand well back. War wasn't always that way. It used to be a face-to-face, eyeball-to-eyeball affair. There may have been archers, sling throwers, and people with javelins who could kill from as far as 50 yards, but most of the fighting was done with swords or cudgels at close range. It was fierce, and it was messy, and, most of all, it was a very personal affair. You or him, one to one, face to face.

Most of us would prefer our spiritual warfare to be of the modern kind. We would like God to equip us with the "Inter Continental Ballistic Missile of the Spirit" or, at the very least, the javelin of the Spirit. We want quick and comfortable fixes for our spiritual problems. We wish that we could sit back in our armchairs and zap our sins as easily as we change the channels on our televisions. Unfortunately, the Christian life doesn't work that way. The final part of the armor of God is not a high-tech, long-range weapon but an old-fashioned, down-and-dirty short sword. This means that if we are going to defeat our temptations and seek to live fruitful, holy lives, then we will need to get up close and personal and set to work with the sword of the Spirit. Like ancient warfare, the struggle for sanctification is a fierce, messy, and intensely personal affair.

THE WORD OF GOD

The sword of the Spirit is the Word of God, the Bible, the place where God speaks to us, uniquely, authoritatively, and decisively. As Paul reminded Timothy, "All Scripture is breathed out by God and profitable for teaching, for reproof, for correction, and for training in righteousness, that the man of God may be complete, equipped for every good work" (2 Tim. 3:16–17). Paul was primarily speaking about the Old Testament, which was the written Word of God that was available in his day. However, the same is true of the New Testament. To stand firm in the Christian life, we need to know, understand, and apply God's Word to our lives.

It is interesting to note that Paul begins and ends his listing of the armor of God with related ideas. He started with the belt of truth, the foundational garment that underlies all the rest. Now he concludes with the sword of the Spirit, the Word of God. The knowledge and application of the truth as it is found in God's Word are quite literally the beginning and end of the story in our struggle to stand firm in the battle for obedience. We may live in an age that declares itself "post-truth" and seems more interested in feelings and experiences than thoughtful analysis and discernment, but this is just one more way in which Christianity is countercultural in our context. Truth matters. Accurate doctrine makes a profound difference. And the sword of the Spirit, the Word of God, is God's truth, given to enable us to stand against the evil one.

Indeed, the sword of the Spirit is the only offensive weapon we have been given with which to deal the devil a decisive blow. All the rest of the Christian's armor is defensive in nature. The belt, the breastplate, the boots, the shield, and the helmet can ward off Satan's blows and defend you against his attacks, but only one thing can really puncture him, and that is the Word of God.

THE SKILLFUL USE OF THE SWORD

Let's look at the sword of the Spirit in action in the hands of the Master, Jesus himself. In Matthew 4 Jesus faced up to the devil in the wilderness. He had been fasting for forty days and forty nights, personally reenacting Israel's wilderness wanderings. During that fast, the devil came to Jesus three times and presented him with three different temptations, each mirroring one of the temptations that Israel faced—and failed—in the wilderness. First, Satan said to Jesus, "If you are the Son of God, command these stones to become loaves of bread" (Matt. 4:3), mirroring Israel's complaining over their lack of food. Next Satan took Jesus to the pinnacle of the temple and said, "If you are the Son of God, throw yourself down" (Matt. 4:6), matching the temptation to Israel to put the Lord to the test. Finally, Satan showed Jesus all the kingdoms of this world and said, "All these

I will give you, if you will fall down and worship me" (Matt. 4:9), mirroring Israel's temptation to false worship.

These situations presented three powerful temptations for Jesus to achieve good ends by the wrong means. There is nothing wrong with wanting food to eat or desiring divine protection, and Jesus had come into the world to rule the nations. But the significant point to notice is how Jesus answered these temptations. Each time he got out his sword. Three times he quoted the Bible to the devil. Turn these stones into bread? The Bible says, "Man does not live by bread alone" (Deut. 8:3). Throw myself down from the temple? The Bible says, "You shall not put the Lord your God to the test" (Deut. 6:16). Worship you? The Bible says, "It is the Lord your God you shall fear" (Deut. 6:13). Stab, stab, stab! And after that, we are told, the devil left him for a season (Matt. 4:11). There is the sword of the Spirit at work, effectively countering temptation.

Now compare that with how you and I typically operate. The devil comes and offers us a juicy temptation. Perhaps it is the opportunity to steal something or to cheat on a test. Perhaps it is the temptation to sleep with a boyfriend before we get married. Or he encourages us to cover up something we've done wrong by lying about it. Or we are tempted to judge others for their sin, or to hate people who have hurt us deeply. How do we respond to Satan? Often, if we even raise any objection at all, we say something like this: "What if I get caught? What would my friends think? What would the people at church think? No. I'd better not." We are answering Satan with human reasons and not with the Word of God. Instead of hitting the devil with a sword, we are batting at him with a pillow. He is much more skilled at debate and argument than we are; after all, he's been doing it for thousands of years. He knows us better than we know ourselves. He'll soon persuade us that we won't get caught, that no one will see, that it must be okay because everyone does it.

But now suppose we had answered him in this way: "The Bible says, 'You shall not steal'" (see Deut. 5:19). "The Bible says, 'Sex is only for those who are married'" (see Gen. 2:24). "The Bible says, 'Speak the truth in love'" (see Eph. 4:15). Those are words of steel that stab temptation in the heart. The devil has no answer for them. Indeed, there is no answer to them. If our desire is simply to know and do what God has revealed in his Word, then there is nothing to debate. Whether we are going to get caught doesn't matter. Whether anyone sees us doesn't matter. Whether everyone is doing it doesn't matter. The issue is, what has God said? The Word of God is a sharp sword that drives away the devil.

SWORD DRILL

A sword in the scabbard is no defense, just as the belt of truth hanging in our closet won't keep our trousers up. So also we need to take out the sword of the Spirit, God's Word, and put it into use. We need to read God's Word and study it, memorize it, immerse ourselves in it, understand what it says and what it means, and believe those things. Otherwise it will do us no good at all. One of Satan's favorite tactics is to question God's Word: "Did God really say . . . ?" He used that tactic successfully on our first parents, Adam and Eve, in the garden of Eden, and found them woefully unprepared (Gen. 3:1). He tried it unsuccessfully on Jesus in the wilderness (Matt. 4:6). But we are often as unprepared as our first parents, either not knowing or not really believing God's Word. We don't want to try to get the hang of our sword during the height of the battle. We want to practice repeatedly with it during the more peaceful times of life so that when the onslaught finally hits, we are fully prepared.

So get into God's Word daily. Find resources that assist you to see how the Bible directs your steps, how it addresses you in your struggles, how it confronts your pet sins, and how it points you back repeatedly to Christ and the gospel. Put it to work in the little challenges so that when great challenges come, you know how it works.

Second, remember whose sword it is. The Spirit is the ultimate author of God's Word and the One who can help us to understand and apply it properly. Before you start to read the Bible, pray. Ask the Holy Spirit to be your teacher, to help you to understand what you are reading and to see how it affects your life. Ask that you may see more clearly how the Bible challenges your particular sins. Ask that as you read, your heart may be stirred up to love Christ more. Ask that your motives may be purified by God's Word.

In John 14 Jesus tells his disciples that the Holy Spirit is himself the Spirit of truth (v. 17). It is his task to teach us all things and to bring to remembrance the things spoken by Jesus, so that we may have peace in a troubled world (v. 26). When you pray, "Holy Spirit, open up your Word to me today; help me to see Jesus and to grow in love for him," you are asking the Spirit to do the very thing he delights to do.

Third, learn from others and share what you are learning with someone else. That's the beauty of Bible studies and community groups—we learn together from God's Word. Such gatherings encourage us to become more filled with the good news of the gospel. The Christian life was never meant to be lived alone but in community. The Bible was not meant to be studied as if we were the first people ever to read it. The Spirit has also been at work in the hearts and minds of those who have gone before us, giving them insights from which we may learn, and he is active in the hearts and minds of other believers, showing them things we may miss. As we read the Bible together with our contemporaries and walk in the light shed upon it by great interpreters from the past, we become accustomed to using our own swords more effectively and skillfully.

THE GARDEN SHEARS OF THE SPIRIT

The Word of God is not only a sword with which we may take on our enemies; it is also a set of garden shears with which God prunes us. If the sword helps us to deal with external challenges, the shears deal with our own superfluous branches. This image comes from Jesus's depiction of the vine and the branches. Jesus is the vine, and we are the branches; we are to abide in him, and his words are to abide in us (John 15:7). That is how we bear abundant fruit for him. As time goes by, however, our hearts get weighed down by all kinds of wrong priorities and desires. Under the pressures of the world in which we live, our energies get channeled into a thousand different directions, and we lose sight of the really important things in life. But God, like a good gardener, prunes us back, cutting out the unnecessary branches so that we can direct our full energies to the really important issues.

God often does this by means of trials. When life is going smoothly, we easily become enamored with the things of this world. However, God loves us too much to allow us to continue in our blindness. In the midst of difficulties, we turn to the Word with a greater hunger, and it confronts us with a vision of the really important things in life. Are you distracted by cares about money? The Bible says, "Man shall not live by bread alone, but by every word that comes from the mouth of God" (Matt. 4:4). Are you distracted by jealousy of what others have? The Bible says:

> One thing have I asked of the LORD,
>   that will I seek after:
> that I may dwell in the house of the LORD
>   all the days of my life,
> to gaze upon the beauty of the LORD
>   and to inquire in his temple. (Ps. 27:4)

Are you distracted by fears? The Bible says, "Do not be anxious, saying, 'What shall we eat?' or 'What shall we drink?' or 'What shall we wear?' . . . Your heavenly Father knows that you need them all. But seek first the kingdom of God and his righteousness, and all these things will be added to you" (Matt. 6:31–33). As the mound of pruned branches grows around our feet, we are pointed back to what really matters: living our lives in the light of God's presence with us and the glorious inheritance that is stored up for us in Christ.

THE SCALPEL OF THE SPIRIT

The Word of God is also a scalpel with which to take on the flesh. The writer to the Hebrews says this:

> The word of God is living and active, sharper than any two-edged sword, piercing to the division of soul and of spirit, of joints and of marrow, and discerning the thoughts and intentions of the heart. And no creature is hidden from his sight, but all are naked and exposed to the eyes of him to whom we must give account. (Heb. 4:12–13)

A sword takes on outside enemies, shears prune back extraneous branches, and a scalpel attacks disease and sickness inside. It is used to perform surgery on the heart. Sometimes we're quick to bring the Bible to bear on other people's problems, and we can quote chapter and verse to show why everybody else is wrong. But the Word of God is not just for taking on our opponents; it is for cleansing our own hearts. God's Word penetrates to the deepest recesses of who we are. As we read the Bible and expose ourselves to it, it cuts us. It convicts us of sin. It points us to duties we'd rather not know about. It challenges us in areas where we are far too comfortable. It digs down into the hidden areas of our soul and lays them bare to God's scrutiny. As it does, it cleanses and purifies us. In the presence of the Word of God, everything is uncovered and laid bare before the eyes of the one to whom we must give account (Heb. 4:13).

This is surely one of the most powerful defenses against sin. To live your life in the light of God's presence, knowing that he sees everything you do, is world changing. Studies have shown that crime doesn't necessarily drop dramatically when courts impose harsher sentences. After all, criminals rarely expect to get caught. Crime drops significantly only when the risk of detection is increased. If people think that they can sin unseen, many will do so; one has to be much more brazen to sin out in the open, in front of everyone. Yet God's Word reminds us that in reality, our whole life is lived in the open before God. There are no hidden corners of our lives where we can squirrel things away out of God's view. He knows and sees all things, and as we expose ourselves to the Word of God, we are convicted of our secret sins as well as our open sins.

This is also a powerful defense against self-righteousness. Many of us compare our outward behavior with those around us and say, "At least, I'm better than him. At least I don't do the terrible things that she does." But the scalpel of the Spirit tears away our self-righteousness, first by uncovering the rottenness that exists deep in the heart of each of us and then by exposing that rottenness to the searching light of God's standard, which is perfection. When we stand before God as our judge, we are left without excuse. He sees the extent to which our lives are filled with wrong actions, wrong thoughts, and wrong words. Fortunately, he often holds us back from living out our worst thoughts. Yet were he to withdraw his hand from supporting us for a moment, we would certainly fall into the grossest kinds of sins. The seeds of all of them are right within our hearts.

But the surgeon's knife doesn't just cut for the sake of making a wound. It cuts to save the whole body by taking out the diseased part. So also the scalpel of the Holy Spirit doesn't just cut us so that God can watch us bleed. The Holy Spirit comes to convict the world not just about sin but about righteousness (John 16:8). That is to say, the Scriptures speak to us not simply about our comprehensively failed attempts to construct a righteousness of our own but also about a new and alien righteousness that we may receive as a free gift of God. God wants to give us a righteousness transplant. In order to do that, of course, he first needs to remove our failing self-righteousness so that we can receive in its place the perfect righteousness of Jesus Christ. There is no room in our heart for both.

When we become Christians, what happens is that we no longer trust in our own good deeds, not even the very best parts of our life. They have all been cut away and exposed by the scalpel of the Spirit so that we may see that even our best actions are diseased by sin. Our motivations for serving people, for doing the right thing, even for reading the Scriptures, are marred with various self-glorying ambitions. For example, we may rise early to read the Bible and pray but be primarily motivated by what our roommate or spouse thinks of us as a result. We may love our wife and family well because it enables us to polish our positive, prideful self-image. We may serve the church unsparingly, addicted to the admiration and praise that our service brings us. How many of the best of our actions actually have the basest of motives? But as we believe in Christ, we receive by grace the free gift of a new, healthy righteousness: the perfect righteousness of Jesus Christ in our place.

JESUS AND THE SWORD OF THE SPIRIT

The sword of the Spirit, the Word of God, is another part of God's armor that he has first worn for us. Once again, the Old Testament provides us with the background. In Isaiah 49:2 the promised servant of the Lord says:

> [The Lord] made my mouth like a sharp sword;
>> in the shadow of his hand, he hid me;
> he made me a polished arrow;
>> in his quiver he hid me away.

In other words, the Lord was preparing his servant to come as a warrior with sharp words of judgment. In the original context, the servant was Israel. They were supposed to be God's faithful servant, equipped by him to bring light to the Gentiles. Yet in Isaiah's time, there was much that needed to be judged and condemned in Israel and Judah. They were not fit to be the Lord's servant, so he had to send his servant to bring light to them as well as to the Gentiles.

This promised servant, the new Israel with a mission to historic Israel, is Jesus himself. Jesus could have entered this world with sharp words of judgment, condemning all those who fall short of perfect righteousness. When they brought him a woman taken in the act of adultery, as one without sin Jesus could himself have cast the first stone (see John 8:1–11). He could have wielded the Word of God as an offensive weapon against us, killing us with it by exposing our failure, brokenness, and sin. In his second coming, Jesus will return as a warrior riding out on a white horse with a sharp sword coming from his mouth with which to judge the nations (Rev. 19:11–16). But in his first coming, Jesus came to wield the Word of God as a scalpel, not as a sword. He came to seek and to save that which is lost, not yet to destroy all his enemies. He came to be a light to the Gentiles and to bring salvation to the ends of the earth (Isa. 49:6), not merely to judge the world.

Such a redemptive mission was far more costly and painful than any war of vengeance would have been. The servant of the Lord in Isaiah lamented:

> I have labored in vain;
>> I have spent my strength for nothing and vanity;
> yet surely my right is with the Lord,
>> and my recompense with my God. (Isa. 49:4)

In order to shine healing light on the nations, the servant would have to be rejected and bruised by his own people. The Spirit's sharp sword of judgment would pierce Jesus's own perfect soul in order to redeem our sinful souls.

Even though the righteousness transplant is free for us, that transplant was not without cost. We must be cut so that our diseased self-righteousness can be removed, but Jesus had to be comprehensively cut off on the cross. The undiseased donor needs to be cut by the surgeon's scalpel as thoroughly as the diseased recipient does: without the shedding of the whole person's blood, the compromised recipient cannot be healed. The perfect servant of the Lord, Jesus, had no disease of sin. He had no wrongdoing that needed to be surgically removed. His entire life was one of perfect love for God and delight in God's glory. But God nevertheless crushed Jesus as if he were thoroughly stained with the dark dye of our foulest sins. The word of God comprehensively condemned Christ on the cross for our sins so that we could be comprehensively justified from our sins through that same cross. Then God raised Jesus up from the dead to prove once and for all that the operation had been a success. The righteousness transplant had taken hold. The scalpel of the Spirit, which wounded Jesus, now makes us whole.

Jesus not only wields the Word of God; he is himself the Word of God. As the Word of God, he spoke the world into existence. As the Word of God, he uniquely reveals to us the Father. As the Word of God, he is God's final communication to this broken and now redeemed world, come to heal the sick, rescue the lost, restore the broken, and lift up the downcast. Have you received the transplant of righteousness that comes through Jesus Christ? It is our only hope of eternal life. The Word of God in its cleansing work serves as a set of shears, a scalpel, and a sword. Ask God to equip you with these three different tools, each one uniquely crafted to help us in the fight against temptation by the world, the flesh, and the devil. All that sanctifying power flows into your life through the work of the Holy Spirit applying his Word. And when you fail and fall, as you often will, the Sword of the Spirit points you back again to the fact that the gospel is still true and Christ's power is still sufficient to keep you safe and bring you at last into your heavenly inheritance.

FOR FURTHER REFLECTION

1. In what ways do we see Satan questioning God's Word in our culture?

2. What is your "sword drill"? How are you practicing the use of God's Word so as to be prepared when you face temptation?

3. How have you experienced God's Word as a sword, a set of garden shears, and a scalpel?

4. How has Jesus wielded the sword of the Spirit in our place?

8

PRAYING ALWAYS

Ephesians 6:18–20

A modern fighter plane is a fearsome weapon, with its combination of cannons, missiles, and bombs. But what happens if the plane suddenly loses electrical power? The armaments still have their theoretical capacity to defend the plane. But because they are no longer under the control of the pilot, their effectiveness is reduced to zero. The plane may still look fearsome, but it is actually worthless.

So it is with the Christian soldier. We've spent seven chapters examining the armor and weapons that have been given to the Christian for his or her struggle against the powers of evil. But it is not enough simply to put on the armor. There will be no powerful reality to your walk with God unless you are in intimate contact with your heavenly Father. That is why Paul concludes his discussion of the Christian's armor by telling the Ephesians that the armor is not enough. The armory needs to be under the control of the pilot; you and I need to be in close contact with God. And the means by which we stay in contact is prayer. Prayer is not so much another weapon that the Christian has been given as it is the means by which all of his or her weaponry is kept effective, under the control and guidance of God.

THE STRUGGLE TO PRAY

Prayer is something with which many of us struggle. I often go through life acting as if I were the hero of the atheist W. E. Henley's poem "Invictus," who declares, "I am the master of my fate, I am the captain of my soul." That attitude is patently delusional in a world where I can't even get my family to bow down and serve my every whim, let alone the wider universe. Yet unless some kind of personal crisis emerges that makes evident the ridiculousness of such a claim, I can canter along independently for days on end, with barely a thought for connecting with God.

When I was younger, I used to be better at blocking out periods of time for prayer in my daily schedule, but I'm not sure that I was actually depending on God. At that point I viewed prayer as one more means to bring my fate under my own mastery and to captain my own soul. I believed that if I spent the right amount of time in the right way in prayer, then God would surely make my life run more smoothly.

Most Christians desire to pray better. The disciples came to Jesus with that very request, and what he gave them was not a sacred set of words to pray verbatim nor a schedule of special times of prayer, but a flexible formula to guide them in their regular daily conversations with God (see Luke 11:9–15).

Likewise, Paul gives no formula or fixed agenda, such as you would find in many religions. Rather he tells them (and us) four things that are to characterize all prayers: we are to pray "at all times in the Spirit, with all prayer and supplication," and we are to do so "with all perseverance, making supplication for all the saints" (Eph. 6:18). This is much more than a technique for prayer or a magic formula to make life go well. It is prayer as the natural outworking of a life lived in utter dependence upon God, who is the true master of our fate and captain of our soul.

PRAYING IN THE SPIRIT

The most important characteristic for our prayers is that they are to be "in the Spirit." We might pray simply to be seen praying, like the Pharisees, who made sure that at the set hours of Jewish prayer, they were standing on the street corners where as many people as possible could see their piety (see Matt. 6:5). We don't pray at street corners, but perhaps the prayers we offer with other Christians are far more passionate and enthusiastic than those we muster up on our own. Or we make sure that others are aware of our long quiet times every morning.

At other times, our prayers might be simply an attempt to get what we want in life: James says, "You do not have, because you do not ask. You ask and do not receive, because you ask wrongly, to spend it on your passions" (James 4:2–3). The context in the book of James suggests that this kind of prayer is a disguised form of coveting. Whereas some fight and steal to get what they want, others misuse prayer as a means of telling God what they think they need—and what he therefore should give them. These are prayers offered in the flesh rather than in the Spirit, prayers offered without any reference to God and his will but simply motivated by the desires of our own idolatries.

Prayer in the Spirit is the outflow and outworking of a relationship with God, which is itself rooted and grounded in his Word. In Ephesians 6 Paul has just identified the Word of God as the sword of the Spirit, so prayer in the Spirit is prayer that flows from understanding that Word. Jude makes the same point when he links "praying in the Holy Spirit" with "building yourselves up in your most holy faith" (Jude 20). A strong relationship with God and praying in the Holy Spirit go hand in hand. Praying in the Spirit is not a mystical experience but rather praying that is prompted and guided by the Holy Spirit.

Almost everyone prays when a crisis hits—when death is near, when you feel out of your depth, before a difficult exam, or while awaiting the results of a medical test. But sometimes there is no real relationship behind those prayers. People are praying not to One they know as their heavenly Father, entrusting the outcome of the situation to his reliable faithfulness, but to a god they don't know, hoping that for some obscure reason he will pull something out of the bag for them. Only those who are God's children can truly pray in the Spirit. Paul tells us in Romans 8:14–16:

> For all who are led by the Spirit of God are sons of God. For you did not receive the spirit of slavery to fall back into fear, but you have received the Spirit of adoption as sons, by whom we cry, "Abba! Father!" The Spirit himself bears witness with our spirit that we are children of God.

If you are a Christian, you have received the Holy Spirit. There are not two different levels of Christians: those who have and those who have not yet received the Holy Spirit. If you are a child of God by faith in Christ, you have received the Spirit. That's why the prayer the Lord taught all of his disciples to pray starts out, "Our Father..." The Lord's Prayer is not a cry to some unknown god. It is a prayer based on a personal relationship with God that enables you to address the Creator of the universe as "Father." The result of that adoption is that whenever you pray, the Spirit testifies that you are part of God's family and therefore have the right to come into God's presence. The Father is delighted that you have come to speak to him. It doesn't always feel that way, of course. Sometimes it feels as if you are simply praying to the ceiling, or you struggle with doubts about God's attitude toward you. But whether you feel it or not, the Bible says that if you are a Christian, you can know that God delights to hear your prayers because his own Spirit indwells your heart.

ARE YOU GOD'S CHILD?

When you pray, do you come to a Father you know and trust, or to a total stranger? The Bible says that Jesus came into the world precisely so that we could have a close, ongoing relationship with God. In John 1:12 we read, "To all who did receive him [Jesus], who believed in his name, he gave the right to become children of God." Of course, that statement presupposes the fact that we're not naturally children of God; indeed, we are quite the reverse until we receive Jesus. God was rightly angry with us for all the wrong things we thought and said and did. Even our best and kindest deeds were defective and unacceptable before a perfect and holy God. By nature, therefore, we *should* feel isolated and alienated from God, shut out of his presence, unable to pray to him. But God's amazing free gift in Jesus Christ is eternal life for all those who believe in him, which includes a new relationship with God as his beloved children. As his children, we have the astonishing privilege of praying to him "in the Spirit," with his Spirit in us understanding our deepest longings and desires and communicating them to God, while at the same time reflecting back to us God's personal love and care.

That's why, just as communication issues in marriage are usually diagnostic of deeper issues in the relationship, problems in prayer are not fundamentally a prayer issue; they are a relational issue. Why am I so slow to pray, and when I do come to pray, why do I find it so hard to focus my mind? It's not because I need to learn better techniques of prayer; it's because I'm not thinking and feeling rightly about who God is and who I am in Christ. I'm not really praying "in the Spirit" to a Father who knows and dearly loves me; I'm acting as if I'm petitioning a distant deity who may or may not be concerned about me.

UNANSWERED PRAYER

How do you respond after you have run to God in prayer during a crisis yet you haven't received the answer for which you've been hoping? You are not healed of your sickness. Your problems are not resolved. Your mother dies. You still can't find a job. You are still alone, without the spouse or child for whom you long, or you are still struggling with a spouse or child who seems determined to wreck your life. Seemingly unanswered prayer can be confusing, especially when the things for which we are praying are good things, such as the salvation of a friend or victory over a particular sin. Yet these are defining moments when you really find out whether you are praying in the context of a real relationship with God or simply because you think prayer might be an effective technique for getting the things you want. Will you become angry at God when he doesn't give you what you want? Will you become despondent about yourself, concluding that God doesn't really love you because you are such a failure? These are common responses when the good desires of our hearts remain unfulfilled.

But the Spirit points us to a different possibility. Remember, Paul penned these words while in prison, quite literally in chains for the sake of the gospel (Eph. 6: 20). Didn't Paul pray to be released? Did Paul not have enough faith when he prayed? Not at all! Rather, this tragic and painful experience was part of God's ongoing loving relationship with Paul, in which God was teaching Paul important lessons that he could learn only in this context. Paul was coming to see that God's power was actually made perfect not in Paul's strength—when he was accomplishing great things through his faith—but rather in his weakness. Paul was learning that God's grace was sufficient for him, even while he sat in a Roman dungeon. Paul understood that he was not merely a Roman prisoner; he was, far more profoundly, "a prisoner of Christ Jesus" (Eph. 3:1).

Can you say that about your unanswered prayer, that you are sick for Christ Jesus, unemployed for Christ Jesus, bereaved for Christ Jesus, alone for Christ Jesus, broken for Christ Jesus? That doesn't mean you can't pray to be healed, or for a job, or for a spouse, of course, but it does impact profoundly how you respond when God doesn't seem to answer your prayers. The problem is not with your lack of faith or with God's lack of power; it is that God has chosen a different path of growth and sanctification for your life right now. It is a call to trust, in weakness and broken-ness, in the God who is your strength and fullness.

Praying in the Spirit gives you a means to tackle the chal-lenges of that lonely and disconsolate path, because, as you pray, you are reminded that you never walk along that pathway alone. God, by his Spirit, always walks it with you. By the Spirit, God was with Paul in that prison cell; by the Spirit, he is with you in the midst of your difficulties and struggles. As you pray in the midst of the darkness, pain, and loneliness, you can ask the Spirit to help you understand and experience God's unfailing love for you. You can ask him to press into your heart the reality that God cares deeply about you and knows so much better than you do what is in your best interests. He loves you far more than you love yourself, and he has demonstrated that love in sending Jesus Christ to die on the cross for you. As you pray, the Spirit constantly reminds you that, whether you can feel it or not, God cannot and won't take that committed love away from you. And as you pray, the Spirit also reminds you that God has the abso-lute right to take away everything else you have, if he knows that that is best for you.

Good parents love their children unconditionally, but that doesn't mean that they give them everything they ask for. Par-ents reserve the right to take away any or all toys if it is in the children's best interests. If you heard that your children's favorite teddy bear or special blanket had been recalled by the manufac-turer because it contained toxic materials, wouldn't you take it away from them? You'd share their sadness and their sense of loss, of course, and you'd cuddle them in their floods of tears, but you'd still take it away because it is in their best interests to do so. The toy they love so much could end up killing them.

So too God sometimes takes away our favorite toys because they are hampering our spiritual growth. He is not being mean or uncaring or punishing us; quite the reverse—it is the most loving thing he could possibly do for us at that moment, something absolutely necessary for our training in righteousness. Those who pray "in the Spirit" thus have a resource to help them in the face of unanswered prayers. They have a relationship with God as their loving heavenly Father. Sometimes, in the Spirit, they may feel the comforting presence of God with them through the darkest hours of life, even when it seems that none of their prayers are being heard or answered. At other times, even though they cannot feel that comforting presence, they are reminded that God's smile still rests upon them, for the sake of Jesus Christ.

PRAYING AT ALL TIMES

The other aspects of prayer that Paul identifies flow from the foundational insight that prayer is rooted in our relationship with God. So Paul tells us that prayers are to be offered on all kinds of occasions. James talks about this in his letter when he says, "Is anyone among you suffering? Let him pray. Is anyone cheerful? Let him sing praise. Is anyone among you sick? Let him call for the elders of the church, and let them pray over him" (James 5:13–14). Prayer should mark your life not just in days of distress and trouble, nor even merely at regular set times in the morning and evening, but also at the most joyful moments of life. In fact, this may provide a diagnostic test of how close your relationship with God really is. When you have a close relationship with someone, you want to interact with him or her regularly, sharing joys as well as sorrows.

In contrast, most of us don't have a close relationship with the federal government. We know it exists and that it influences our lives in many ways. In moments of severe difficulty, we may go to our senator or congressman to make specific petitions and requests, saying, "Please intercede on our behalf in Washington," or, "Do something about this or that terrible problem that faces our nation." We may get angry and write letters of complaint when the government is not willing or able to give us what we want. But in moments of personal triumph, such as when we pass an exam or when we get a promotion or get married or when our child takes her first faltering steps, our first thought is not normally to share a picture with our congressman. We sense that he really isn't interested in that. Yet these are precisely what good parents want to hear about.

When my children come home, I want to hear about their day—what was good, what was bad, what was indifferent. It doesn't have to be of earthshattering importance. I'm interested because I'm Dad. My children can and do text me about anything and everything at any hour of the day or night. In fact, I'd consider that I'd failed as a parent if the only time my children talked to me was when they wanted my help. I want them to know that I love and care for them. And that is the relationship that God desires to have with you and me. He wants us to pray on all kinds of occasions because that is part of having a childlike relationship with him. Children don't store up their news and requests for a special thirty-minute time at the beginning and end of the day; they burst into their parents' presence as soon as they have something to share!

So too God desires you to share your trials and joys with him moment by moment throughout the day, delighting with him in the good stuff and sharing the minor struggles and inconveniences, not just the terrible traumas of life. You can shoot off brief thanksgivings and requests throughout the ups and downs of daily living, acknowledging moment by moment the reality of God's interest in your life. The more you see God's hand at work throughout the day, the more you will want to talk to him about it—the accidents you almost had that he prevented; the test you should have failed but didn't; the random loving thoughts that come into your mind that you know aren't from you; yes, even the parking space that opened up just when you needed it. As your eyes open to your heavenly Father, you begin to see more and more of his constant activity on your behalf.

EVERY KIND OF PRAYER AND SUPPLICATION AT ALL TIMES

Your prayers should also be wide-ranging. Nothing is out of bounds. Our prayers are often limited by our small imaginations and little faith. We don't pray for big things because we don't really believe in our heart of hearts that God can or will do them. We pray for small sinners to become Christians, but not for really big sinners. We pray for victory over small sins in our lives, but we don't know how to pray about those big, ingrained sinful habits. We pray for change in our small corner of the universe but not in the country at large or throughout the world. Instead of praying with *all* kinds of prayers and requests, we pray with *small* kinds of prayers and requests.

Or, alternatively, we pray in very large and general terms for the universe but never engage with the specific details of life. We don't think God is interested in the minutia of our experience. Let Paul challenge your vision! We serve a great and mighty God who is involved in the tiny details of life. He sustains every aspect of the vast cosmos day by day. He causes kingdoms to rise and kingdoms to fall, while at the same time supervising the lifecycle of each and every chipmunk in our garden. And, astonishingly, he chooses to work through our prayers.

One way to increase the scope of your prayers is to study the great prayers of the Bible. Think about Jesus's High Priestly Prayer in John 17, for example. On the night before he died, Jesus prayed for several very specific things. First, he prayed that the Father would glorify him. So too, we can pray that the Father would glorify Jesus Christ in and through our lives—in our strength or in our weakness, in our health or in our sickness, in our abundance or in our poverty. He also prayed for his disciples, and those who would believe through their witness, that the Father would keep them safe and united. So too we can pray for ourselves and for our churches that we would be kept safe and united in Christ.

Jesus also prayed that the Father would sanctify his disciples in the truth, so we can pray that God would grow us in our daily holiness and knowledge of the truth. We can pray that the Spirit, who inspired his Word, would make us knowledgeable and effective in living lives in accordance with that Word. And Jesus prayed that ultimately we might be with him in heaven to see his glory. So we can pray for God's sustaining power to enable us, weak and broken as we are, to persevere faithfully throughout the course of our earthly lives; and we can pray for God to sustain others who are equally weak and faltering. As we ponder this prayer of Jesus, we may learn new petitions and requests to bring before the Father.

Our prayers are not simply to be big and small; they are also to be wide, ranging around the world, praying for all the saints. In many countries the church is growing very rapidly, and it needs our prayers that it will remain true to the Bible. In other areas, Christians are a persecuted minority and need our prayers that they will stand firm in what they believe. We also need the prayers of our brothers and sisters around the world. If even Paul needed the prayers of the Ephesians so that he could be faithful in proclaiming the gospel, how much more do contemporary pastors and missionaries around the globe need prayer?

Our calling is not to pray just for pastors and missionaries either, as if it were only "super-Christians" who really need our prayers. We need to pray for *all* the saints. Paul regularly told the churches to whom he was writing that he prayed for them. Will you be able to say one day to multitudes of people you've never met, "I prayed for you"? Nor is it just the saints around the world; there are believers right around the corner in your family, in your church, and in your community who need your persistent prayers.

THE ONE WHO INTERCEDES FOR US

Some of the books I have read about prayer left me feeling crushed and inadequate, unable to conceive how anyone could pray sufficiently. But if we circle back to the idea of prayer as the outworking of a relationship, it becomes a different story. If prayer is simply responding to the promptings of the Spirit to cry out to my heavenly Father with thanksgiving, with requests, with intercessions, and with sighs of confession and repentance, then all of a sudden it doesn't seem so hard. If you think of praying in the Spirit at all times, with all kinds of prayers, persistently for all of the saints, as a job description, it will wear you out. But for us as children of the great king, it is simply living life in the presence of our king. It is lifting our hearts and minds and voices regularly to him in petition and praise as the Spirit leads.

What is more, prayer is not a task we carry out alone. Jesus lived the perfect prayer life that you and I never can, constantly communicating with his Father, constantly interceding for others, and even praying for future followers like you and me. What is more, he is still praying for you. In Hebrews 7:25 we read that Christ ever lives beside the throne of God the Father to make intercession for his people. The Spirit too intercedes for us and with us; in Romans 8:26 Paul tells us that when we don't know how or what to pray, the Spirit himself intercedes for us with groanings too deep for words. With company like that praying with and for us, how will the Father not give us exactly what is best? Jesus's constant prayer covers our weak, inconsistent, and often half-hearted praying.

So pray in the Spirit, as the outflow of your relationship with your heavenly Father. Pray in season and out of season on all sorts of occasions for all kinds of prayers and requests, persistently for all the saints. Then indeed, as Paul prays for the Ephesians, peace will grip your hearts along with love and faith. And the grace of God will constantly be with you in the midst of the fiercest battle, along with all those who love our Lord Jesus Christ.

FOR FURTHER REFLECTION

1. How do you sometimes pray wrongly?

2. How do you normally react to unanswered prayers? To answered prayers?

3. When have you needed to say, "This suffering is for Christ Jesus?" How did you deal with that situation?

4. How do you remind yourself to pray at all times with all kinds of requests?

5. How is Jesus's continuous prayer for you an encouragement?

ACKNOWLEDGMENTS

This study of the Christian's armor has been in development for a long time. It began in seed form in a series preached at our first church plant, Redeemer Presbyterian Church, Oxford, England, in the summer of 1994. Since then, it has been repreached in Aliso Creek and Fallbrook, California, and at Christ Presbyterian Church, Grove City, Pennsylvania, and in Glenside, Pennsylvania. The idea dates back further still, however, in the Puritan William Gurnall's massive seventeenth-century classic *The Christian in Complete Armor*, which I read in seminary. I am indebted to the breadth of Gurnall's vision (though my book is considerably shorter and more focused), and to the support of the various congregations along the way that helped encourage me as a younger preacher. My focus throughout has been seeking to learn how to preach *Christ* from all the Scriptures, New Testament as well as Old.

In pursuit of that goal, I have frequently been helped immensely by the penetrating questions and insights of my wife, Barb. She has a remarkable ability to point the way from any passage to the active and passive obedience of Christ, seeking out the way in which this particular part of God's Word is *good news* to the hearers. I have learned so much from her and certainly couldn't do what I do without her patient support and keen understanding.

Lydia Brownback helped greatly to make the manuscript more readable, and many others at Crossway were involved in the production process. Thank you! It has been a pleasure to work with you.

Finally, my children—Wayne, Jamie, Sam, Hannah, Rob, and Rosie—each heard these sermons at least once growing up. It is my prayer that the message that Christ has worn the armor of God in our place will continue to be an encouragement to them in the ongoing trials and difficulties of this earthly battlefield.

GENERAL INDEX

Adam, temptation of, 28, 33, 93
affliction: and hope, 83; produces
        perseverance and character, 83
armor of God, 10, 16–17; under
        control of pilot, 104; worn by
        Christ, 17, 22, 33, 82
assurance, 81–82, 88

Babylon, idols of, 54
belt of truth, 16, 25–36
besetting sin, 85
Bible: convicts us of sin, 97; as
        system of truth, 30–32
Bible reading, as putting on truth, 28
Bible studies, 94
Bierce, Ambrose, 66
boldness of faith, 84–85
breastplate of righteousness, 17,
        37–49
brokenness, 21, 110

Canons of the Synod of Dordt, 18n4
certainty of salvation, 80–81
Chesterton, G. K., 31
children of God, 107–8
Christian life: as battle, 10, 21–22;
        in community, 94–95; as daily
        struggle, 47–48; and Word of
        God, 90
Christian soldier, 12; walk with
        God, 103

clinging to God, 68
clothing and dress, 9
commandments, 71
community groups, 94
confidence, 81–82
coveting, 105

darkness, 12
despair, 82–83
devil: attacks of, 26; hates truth, 28;
        lies of, 46–47; schemes of, 13;
        temptation from, 92–93; as
        very real opponent, 10
discouragement, 82
divine warrior, 39–41, 78
doctrine, 30–31
doubt, 83
Dr. Who (television program), 13

Edinburgh, 25
eternal life, 80, 108
evangelism, 53, 61–62
evil, 10–11

faith: built on truth, 70–72; lays
        hold of God's power, 73–74;
        points to God's promises,
        72–73; rooted in reality, 65–66;
        as shield, 68–70; and trust in
        goodness of God, 75
faithfulness to truth, 33

fears, 96

feet shod with gospel readiness, 17, 32–33

freedom of the gospel, 55–56

garden shears, Word of God as, 95–96, 101

God: comforts his people, 56–58; love of, 46; on our side, 70; power in weakness, 109–10; power of, 74; prunes as a gardener, 95–96; reigns, 54–56; reigns in evangelism, 61; as shield, 67–68, 75; sovereignty of, 69–70

good news of peace, 58–61

gospel: and freedom from false gods, 55–56; as word of truth, 27

gospel of peace, 59–61

Gurnall, William, 119

heaven, 86–87

Heidelberg Catechism, 15

hell, 86

helmet of salvation, 17, 77–88

Henley, W. E., 104

heralds of the gospel, 43–54

Hezekiah, 19

Holy Spirit: and the Bible, 94; intercession of, 116; and prayer, 105–7; remakes into image of Christ, 45; sanctifying work of, 22; as Spirit of truth, 94; and spiritual growth, 17–19

hope, 79; gives boldness, 84–85; and holy living, 86–87; for Israel, 57; not a vague optimism, 79; and resistance to sin, 85

idols, 54–55

imputed righteousness of Christ, 44, 49

"in Christ," 43

"Invictus" (poem), 104

Isaiah, on redemption and hope, 60

Israel: hardness of heart, 56–57; hope for, 57

Jesus Christ: cut off on the cross, 101; faithfulness to the truth, 33–35; herald of good news, 58–59, 62–63; High Priestly Prayer, 114; intercession of, 116; perfect prayer life of, 116; prayer as great High Priest, 75; as promised servant, 100; resisted sin and Satan, 16; resurrection of, 101; righteousness of, 82; secured our peace, 59; suffered the anguish sin deserved, 72; temptation from Satan, 17, 34, 91–92, 93; took on our sin, 41–42; used sword of the Spirit, 91, 99; as the Word of God, 101; wore armor of God, 17, 22, 33, 82

judgmentalism, 15

justification, 47

knowledge and application of the Word of God, 90

Lord's Prayer, 107

materialism, 11

memorizing the Word of God, 93

modern warfare, 89, 103

momentary light affliction, 83

money, 96

nations, comfort for, 56–58

new creation, 43

Newton, John, 19n5, 20

Niles, D. T., 62

object of faith, 65

Paul: on power in weakness, 109; on
    prayer, 113–15; as prisoner of
    Christ Jesus, 109
peace, 57–61
perseverance, in prayer, 105
Pharisees, prayer of, 105
"post-truth," 91
prayer, 103–16; for all the saints,
    115; at all times, 111–13; and
    relationship with God, 111–13,
    115–16; in the spirit, 105–7,
    108, 111; as struggle, 104–5; as
    wide-ranging, 113–15
pride, 15, 44
prodigal son, parable of, 44
promises of God, 72, 75
protection, 82–83

readiness of the gospel of peace, 52
reading the Word of God, 93, 94
reconciliation with God, 42–43
relationship with God, 106, 107–8,
    111–13, 115–16
resurrection, 14, 75
righteousness: credited to our ac-
    count, 42; of Christ, 35, 44, 48,
    98; of God, 40–41, 79; of one's
    own, 38–40, 48
righteousness transplant, 98–99,
    100–101
rulers, authorities, and cosmic
    powers, 10–11

salvation, accomplished by Christ,
    82
sanctification, 14–16, 18, 22, 47
Satan: lies of, 33–36; power of, 20;
    questioned the Word of God,
    93; as roaring lion, 12; tempta-
    tions of Jesus, 17, 34, 91–92,
    93; as tempter, 13, 28, 34

scalpel, Word of God as, 96–99, 101
Scripture, breathed out by God, 90
self-righteousness, 44, 97–98, 101
servant of the Lord, 41, 99–101
shears. *See* garden shears
shield, 67–68
shield of faith, 65–75
sin: as besetting, 85; conviction of,
    97; as greatest enemy, 78; and
    rebellion, 71; struggle with, 18;
    warrants death, 39
spiritual: failures, 20–21; forces,
    11; growth, 17–19; makeover,
    10; warfare, 89–90; workahol-
    ics, 61
studying the Word of God, 93
suffering servant, 41
sword drill, 93–94
sword of the Spirit, 17, 89–102; as
    offensive weapon, 91

temptations, 20, 28, 34
Ten Commandments, 80
Tolkien, J. R. R., 12
training in righteousness, 111
trials, 83, 95–96
trust, 75, 110
truth, 26–27, 90–91; faith built on,
    70–72; victorious over Satan's
    lies, 36

unanswered prayer, 108–11
unbelief, 74–75
union with Christ, 42–43

vine and branches, 95

warfare, 89
watchmen, 53
weakness, 19–22, 109–10
Westminster Confession of Faith,
    17–18n4, 20
Word of God, 90–91; as truth, 27

SCRIPTURE INDEX

Genesis
2:16–17 28
2:24 93
3:1 ....28, 93
15 17
15:1 67

Exodus
20:3 71
20:12 71
20:13 71
20:14 71
20:15 71
20:17 71

Deuteronomy
5:19 93
6:13 92
6:16 92
8:3 92

2 Chronicles
32:21 19

Psalms
3:3 67
19:7–11 29–30
23:4 73
27:4 96
28:7 67

91:3–6 67–68
119:114 67

Proverbs
30:5 67

Isaiah
1:8 57
6:1–7 60
6:8 60
6:9–13 57
11:1 57
11:5 ....17, 33
19:23–25 57
40:1–11 57
49:2 ....17, 99
49:4 100
49:6 ....58, 100
51:5–8 78
52:7 ....17, 52
52:10 40
53:5 42
53:12 ....40, 42
59 39
59:2 40
59:16 40
59:17 ....17, 38, 78, 82
59:19 40
61 58
64:6 40

Zechariah
3............................42

Matthew
4:3.........................91
4:4........................34, 96
4:6.........................91, 93
4:7.........................34
4:9.........................34, 92
4:10.......................34
4:11.......................92
5:21–28...................71
6:5.........................105
6:31–33...................96
16:24......................21
27:39–43..................35
27:46......................42
28:19–20..................62

Mark
5:22–42...................59

Luke
4:18–19...................58
5:12–13...................59
11:9–15...................104
15:11–32..................44
22:31–32..................75
23:46......................36

John
1:12.......................107
3............................18
4:1–26....................59
8:1–11....................100
8:44.......................28
11:1–44...................14
14:17......................94
14:6.......................27
14:26......................94
15:7.......................95
16:8.......................98
17.........................114

19:21–22..................35
19:30......................36

Acts
4:12.......................27
19:18–19..................12

Romans
6:14.......................85
6:23.......................39
7:24.......................21, 86
8:1.........................43
8:14–16...................106
8:26.......................116
8:28–31...................30
8:38.......................73
10:13–15..................53

1 Corinthians
6:11.......................47
15:19......................66

2 Corinthians
4:17.......................83
5:17.......................43, 45
5:19.......................42
5:21.......................41

Ephesians
1............................55
1:4–6......................16
1:13.......................27
1:19.......................14
2............................70
2:4.........................71
2:10.......................45
2:11–22...................58
3:1.........................109
4:15.......................93
4:21.......................27
6............................33
6:10.......................13, 19
6:10–11...................14

6:12......................10, 11
6:15......................52
6:16......................66
6:18......................105
6:20 109

Philippians
1:6.........................18, 83
2:12–13................18
2:13......................16

1 Thessalonians
5:8.........................79

2 Timothy
3:16–17 90

Hebrews
4:12–13................96
4:13......................97
5:8.........................82
5:9.........................82
7:25......................116

11:1......................72
12:2......................82

James
1:2–3....................83
1:22–25................27–28
4:2–3 105
5:13–14 111

1 Peter
3:15......................79
5:8.........................12

1 John
2:16......................34
4:4 ....14, 73
5:11–12 80
5:13......................80

Jude
20 106

Revelation
19:11–16................100